VISIONS *of* SUGARPLUMS

VISIONS *of*
SUGARPLUMS

Twenty Years Behind the Beard

Jeff Schatzer (signature)

JEFFERY L· SCHATZER

BIG BELLY BOOKS
P. O. Box 1127
Bellaire, MI 49615
www.bigbellybooks.com

Names: Schatzer, Jeffery L., author
Title: Visions of sugarplums : twenty years behind the beard / Jeffery L. Schatzer.
Description: Bellaire, MI : Big Belly Books, [2016]
Identifiers: ISBN: 978-0-9749554-5-2 | LCCN: 2016948776
Subjects: LCSH: Schatzer, Jeffery L. | Santa Claus. | Santa Claus—Fiction. | Christmas stories. | BISAC: Holidays/Memoir.
Classification: LCC: GT4992 .S338 2016 | DDC: 394.2663—dc23

Printed in the United States of America

Cover photo by Shelly Bartosek

Cover and page design by Mary Jo Zazueta
tothepointsolutions.com

To my loving wife, Deborah.
Her abiding faith, endless support, and
tireless efforts have given life to this dream.

Contents

VISIONS of
SUGARPLUMS

Photo by Don Rutt (fabulousfaces.com)

Introduction

Photo by Don Rutt (fabulousfaces.com)

Cold north winds and billowing dark clouds tell me it's time to get ready for Christmas once again. While Santa's elves and helpers are busy preparing everything from toys to wrappings and candy, I spend my spare time thinking about my most favorite memories. You see, many people believe it is the children who love to see Santa; and I'm sure that is true. However, I love to visit with the children every bit as much as they like to see Santa.

For me, there is nothing like a cherished memory to get into the holiday spirit.

A very long time ago, I decided to keep a diary of my experiences while portraying Santa Claus. The Christmas season is so busy and passes so quickly, it would be easy for me to forget some of them, even the ones I enjoyed most; so I started to write them down.

My "Santa" diary isn't a fancy book. It is mostly scraps of paper, a few pictures that children have drawn for me over the years, and notes that carry me back to many special moments. There isn't enough space in an entire library to share all of my memories with you. In fact, some are so special and personal, I don't share them with anyone.

I hope the recollections and short stories in this book bring you a measure of joy and happiness. I begin this collection with a cherished recollection; its telling brings the memory fresh to mind. Moreover, it is the story of a child with a good heart and a kind spirit.

Believe Forever,

Santa Claus

A Child's Heart

Photo by Don Rutt (fabulousfaces.com)

Dan is a talented, professional photographer.
His wife, Kay, is a successful real estate agent.
They are wonderful, salt-of-the-earth people.
Although we have lived far from each other
for years, their son, Danny, and his kind
heart, roll through my thoughts every year at
Christmastime.

Years ago, it just so happened that Dan and I
were working on a project together. During the

course of conversation, he told me about his son's annual ritual of writing a letter to Santa on Thanksgiving Day. Once Danny finished the message and sealed it in an envelope, the family marched it outside. His heartfelt wishes were placed in the mailbox, the flag was lifted, and the letter was sent on its way to the North Pole.

Magically, after our conversation, Danny's annual appeals came into my possession before the Christmas season.

Many of my December weekends and evenings are devoted to visiting with children as Santa Claus. Danny's letter stayed with me throughout the season, snuggly tucked inside my wool vest. I did not know when I would run into him, but I knew we would meet at some point.

One winter evening, just before Christmas, I experienced one of my most delightful memories: I looked up and there in front of me stood Dan, Kay, and Danny. Danny stepped forward and wrote his name in the registry next to my chair. I pulled the envelope out of my vest and said, "Danny, I just got your letter. Can we read it together?"

His eyes sparkled and he nodded enthusiastically. As he approached me, I held the unopened letter in my hand. First we talked about school and his favorite sports; then I opened his letter and we began to explore each word and line. His father worked on the fringes to capture our discussion firsthand through his lens. Kay, the proud mother, stood nearby watching it all. Both parents glowed.

Danny's smile could warm anyone's heart. His broad, toothy grin was wide and genuine. When we first met, he had short, brown hair and bright eyes. He was respectful and well spoken. His soft, almost shy, voice and his manners clearly told me that he was a fine young man. Dan and Kay had every right to be proud of their son.

Over the years, we've had many great conversations, but what made my moments with Danny most memorable were his letters to Santa. (At the end of the season, I would return Danny's letters to his dad. To this day, Dan and Kay still have those letters.) Danny's wishes were always centered on others rather than self. As I recall, one message conveyed that he was happy and wanting for nothing. However, he did ask if Santa could leave a soccer ball for some children in a poor region of the world.

I discovered that Danny and his family volunteered their time to help the poor on islands outside of the United States. Those experiences have given Danny a different perspective on life and shaped his thinking.

Every year many children request gifts for others—some of their requests are quite thoughtful ... health for loved ones, food for the poor, homes for the homeless, world peace, and saving homeless puppies—I have rarely experienced the kindness and humanity Danny exhibited in his letters. Danny's letters to Santa always stood out from the others.

A photograph Dan took of Danny and me is found on the last page of my book *The Bird in Santa's Beard*. It is a piece of photographic artistry that quickly carries me back to those magical moments with the most kindhearted young man I've ever met: Danny.

Now, on to how this whole thing got its start ...

The Charles W. Howard
Santa Claus School

Doug called me in August of 1996. His questions were short and to the point. "What are you doing in early fall? Do you have a few days of vacation time?"

My answers were equally short and to the point. "Nothing and Yes."

"Good," he replied. "You and I are going to Santa Claus school together."

We both had a good laugh at the idea, never expecting it would be a life-changing event.

The date was set and deposits secured our involvement. The weeks flew by and before long, Doug and I were sitting on hard wooden benches at the beginning of three delightful days of classes with sixty or so other potential Santas from around the world.

The Charles W. Santa Claus School in Midland, Michigan, is a treat for the senses. Multiple sets of electric trains circled the room. Beautiful decorations and wrapped boxes were everywhere. Animated elves twisted and turned. One elf even played the piano. Along with this visual spectacle, colored bright lights and happy holiday sounds filled the building.

The first question people ask me when they discover I attended Santa Claus school is: What could you possibly do over three days?

Our Santa syllabus included:

+ Dress, hygiene, apparel, and makeup
+ Interview and on-camera practice in a television studio
+ Singing ("Rudolph the Red-Nosed Reindeer," "Jingle Bells," "We Wish You a Merry Christmas," etc.)
+ Dancing, including a bit on ballroom dancing for Mr. and Mrs. Claus
+ Meeting with groups of preschoolers (for practice)
+ Visit a major toy retailer to review the hottest toys of the coming season
+ Sign language lessons
+ Storytelling tips
+ Santa in the history of the arts—a fascinating class conducted by a professor of art history

While the classes were informative, perhaps the greatest insights came from interacting with the other individuals who also portrayed the Spirit of Christmas. The following are a few stories about the characters I encountered at Santa Claus school:

Little Devin

Neither Doug nor I had any idea of what to expect our first morning of class at the school. After introductions, our hosts—Tom and his wife, Holly—began to lead us in singing Christmas songs while offering highlights of the rich history of the school.

Tom was between thoughts in his lecture when we heard a big-throated motorcycle turn the corner and pull up outside. A moment after the loud twin engine sputtered to a stop, the huge wooden door behind us flew open, and a mountain of a human being stepped forward. He was so huge he barely fit inside the door frame. Long, black hair hung in ringlets to his shoulders. Two days of stubble and a goatee against a ruddy complexion cast a sinister look. Patches of all sorts and sizes were sewn on his worn leather jacket, and a road-beaten leather saddlebag was draped over one hand.

The newspaper headline flashed in my mind:

60 SANTAS BEATEN TO A PULP
ENRAGED GANG MEMBER HELD
AS PERSON OF INTEREST

Tom broke the awful silence. "Look everybody, Little Devin is here."

An immense, joyful smile covered the giant's face. "Hi, Santa," he replied to Tom. "And hi, everybody. I'm Devin."

The Santas-to-be replied in unison, like we were in group therapy. "Hi, Devin."

Devin apologized for being late, and then approached Tom. After he gave Tom a warm hug, Devin explained his circumstances:

Devin drives a custom, chopped, Harley Davidson Softail. His bike has mini ape hanger handlebars with studded grips. Glittering chrome sparkles in the wheels and exhaust pipes. Above his 1200 cc twin engine rests the coolest aspect of his custom work: The gas tank has a mad clown with flowing flames of hair painted on each side. Above the freaky looking clown are the words: Mama's Nightmare.

He left home at 6:00 a.m. in order to arrive on time for the 8:30 a.m. class. Although he allowed plenty of time for the trip, Devin was slowed by construction. Running late, he picked up speed along the two-lane highway. About midway across the state, flashing red lights in his rearviews caught his attention.

Devin pulled over and shut down the engine as the cruiser pulled in behind. He watched in his mirrors as the officer opened the door of the cruiser and engaged his radio. Devin could tell the officer was calling in his license plate number. After a squawked reply over the radio, the officer approached Mama's Nightmare.

"Good morning, sir." The officer said. "Do you have any idea how fast you were traveling this morning?"

Devin answered politely. "Good morning to you, sir. I'm sorry to tell you that I don't exactly know how fast I was going."

The officer was taken aback. "I have you clocked at eighty-five. Do you know what the speed limit is on this stretch?"

"It's fifty-five miles per hour in this stretch," Devin answered. "I'm sorry, I was just in a hurry."

The officer asked Devin where he was heading. Devin replied, "I'm running late for Santa Claus School."

That simple and truthful statement of fact began a flurry of questions and rebuttals. You can easily imagine the police officer's skepticism. An exchange of "There is no such thing!" followed by "Yes, there is!" preceded much discussion before the officer made a challenging offer. "If you can prove it, I won't write you up and you're out of here with a warning."

Devin climbed off Mama's Nightmare and started to open one of his saddlebags. The officer tensed as the biker unbuckled the strap and lifted the flap.

Before I reveal what was in Devin's saddlebags, let me tell you about the individual. He worked in the coal yard of a power plant. Devin lived near the shores of Lake Michigan at the western edge of the Lower Peninsula. Every year, he gathered hundreds of small nuggets of coal, made little green sacks from felt, and filled these sacks with chunks of black nuggets. Finally, he tied off each bundle with a gold ribbon.

During the year, Devin works with bike clubs across the state to raise money to sponsor a special Christmas party for needy children. The children are fed a healthy meal. Following lunch, they have the opportunity to visit with Santa and gifts are given to each child.

The officer backed up and Devin raised his hands and stepped away from his bike. He spoke softly. "My proof is in the saddlebag. Look for yourself."

The officer had Devin put his hands on the hood of the cruiser to secure him before returning to the saddlebag and opening it cautiously. His hand wrapped around a small sack, which he removed. The deputy took the item back to the cruiser, opened it, and examined the contents while he sat in his cruiser. Then he went back to Mama's Nightmare and emptied the contents of both saddlebags. After a thorough inspection, the officer returned to his cruiser, closed the door, and got on his radio.

Outside the vehicle, it was difficult for Devin to pick out much of the conversation between the officer and dispatch. Cars slowly passed by, scornful eyes looking out at a scene of what was imagined to be a drug bust or the apprehension of a major criminal.

The officer placed the lump of coal back in its green felt bag and retied the gold ribbon. He stepped out of his cruiser, squared himself, adjusted his hat, and assumed a tall stance. The officer stepped forward and spoke with an air of authority decorated with the hint of a smile.

"Dispatch tells me that she read about a Santa school going on in Midland. Are you saying that you are a student?"

"Yes, sir," Devin answered.

The officer raised the bag of coal and asked, "Sir, what exactly is this?"

Devin smiled meekly, "I bag lumps of coal for students at the Santa Claus school. They show them to boys and girls who are on the naughty list." Devin let the idea sink in before he continued. "That one is yours."

After a hearty laugh, the officer gave Devin a stern warning about following the speed limit. To make certain the law was obeyed, Mama's Nightmare was followed closely by the cruiser ... at the speed limit ... until they crossed the county line.

Crossing the "Yard"

Our first day at Charles W. Howard Santa Claus School was focused on how to dress, followed by instructions on how to make a proper entrance. Essentially, Santa is to enter with a hearty HO! HO! HO! Once he gathers the children around him, he assures them that they've been pretty good this year. Then, after a few minutes of visiting, Santa makes a classy exit.

On the second day of class, we were given the opportunity to practice our skills on local preschoolers and kindergarteners. Busses shuttle excited youngsters to the Santa House every thirty minutes. A different individual in the persona of Santa visited with different groups of children. In the afternoon, each student's performance was assessed by the entire class.

As I mentioned, the Santa school is conducted in a magical place. The outside looks like an enchanted chalet.

A bell tower with animated figurines rings on the hour and matches the stirring majesty of the interior of the house, which has everything—except a changing room for Santa.

When I attended the school, we changed into our Santa regalia in a building next to the Santa House, which just happened to also serve as the county jail. The first day I crossed the yard between the county building and the Santa House dressed as Santa, a voice from above stopped me in my tracks.

"Hey! Santa Claus! Get me out of jail!" an inmate in the holding cells on the second floor called down.

In reply, I gave what has become one of my favorite responses: "Improve your behavior!"

I have wonderful memories of my first Santa school experience, nearly twenty years ago. However, to this day, I still laugh at the thought of my exchange with the incarcerated. And, whenever adults call out and ask me for new cars, high-end boats, whatever ... I continue to use the response I used that October morning: "Improve your behavior!"

I use it hundreds of times every year.

Sparky the Clown

A surprising number of the Santa school students were professional clowns. Some clowned for children's parties, others were circus clowns looking for a source of income during the off season. In addition to being Santa for a major sports team, Sparky worked for Ringling Brothers Circus for years.

I had never met a circus clown before, so I took advantage of the opportunity to satisfy my curiosity. After I introduced myself, I politely asked, "Sparky, have you ever been in one of those little cars full of clowns?"

Sparky sat up straight. His eyes widened. He punctuated his first words with the index finger of his right hand. "Yes, sir, I did.

"Since I was the smallest, see ..." he began, "they put me in the car first. One time, see, they put a Shetland pony in the car before I climbed inside. Then, ten other clowns piled on top of me and the little horse. One of the clowns grabbed the steering wheel and we took off for a few runs around the center ring."

I could see the memory of that moment racing across Sparky's mind.

"After our circular tour, the car came to a stop in the center ring. That's when all hell broke loose."

Sparky leaned in closer to me as he retold the event with great gusto and more than a little drama. "Once the car stopped, the circus master shot off a cannon. As gun smoke filled the air, a clown would pop out of the car and the band would strike up the traditional 'Ta-Dah.'"

His voice hushed as he unburdened himself with detail. "Nobody had any idea that loud noises scare the hay out of horses, even little horses. What's worse, the pony nibbled me every time the cannon shot off!"

Sparky held up his scarred forearm. "Each time the cannon boomed, that little horse would corncob me." He then mimicked the action of the pony nibbling up and down his arm. "Then the darn thing started kicking." His face fell at the wretched memory. "That's the last time I'll ever be in a clown car with a Shetland pony," he stated matter-of-factly.

Hans

Tom and Holly hosted a chili supper for the Santa school participants. I took a seat next to an interesting looking gentleman who was sitting alone on the couch. I was stunned to discover Hans was the vice mayor of one of Greenland's largest cities. Over the course of our conversation, we talked about Greenland's native culture. During our conversation, he emphasized the significance his culture places on singing.

Hans also told me about going through customs when he entered the United States and realized that he might have a problem on his hands. His prized Santa suit was trimmed with real polar bear fur and such items were not permitted to enter the United States because of the animal's endangered status.

Every minute seemed like an hour as Hans waited for his bags to clear US Customs. Would his suit be confiscated? Would he face jail time or a severe fine? Would he make his connecting flight to Midland? Eventually, he heard his name called over the loudspeaker. Hans presented himself to an agent and was escorted out of the holding area and down a sterile-looking hallway that led to a large assembly room. The room was ringed with customs agents and his bags were lying opened in the center of the circle. After being led to his bags, the agent turned and smiled sheepishly.

"We'd all like to see you in your suit," she said, "if that's okay."

The agents respectfully turned their backs while Hans climbed into his gear. Once ready, he told them to turn around. The agents stood in awe when they saw him. Their faces lit up and they became children again, if just for a moment. My new friend then took an additional step. He told them about the significance of song in the his culture. To their surprise and delight, he sang a rare and sacred song.

Needless to say, Hans made it safely through customs and out of the country upon his departure. Never once was he questioned about the possession of polar bear fur.

Saint Nicholas and Schmutzli

Students from overseas enhanced the learning and cultural diversity of the Santa school. Like the rest of us, they came to learn and share. One particular year, students and alumni had an opportunity to learn about Switzerland's Christmas customs. In that country, St. Nicholas is a revered character. He is dressed in white robes; the tall, white hat of a bishop crowns his head. According to their legends, St. Nicholas lives in a cabin deep in the forest with a character named Schmutzli.

Schmutzli is typically smaller in stature than St. Nicholas, somewhat elfin in size. In some areas of Switzerland,

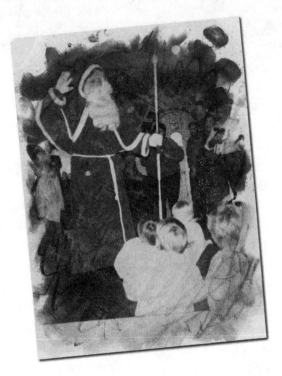

children believe Schmutzli stalks the streets at night with a bundle of switches flung on his back, and he goes about punishing children who misbehave. In other areas of the country, Schmutzli speaks to the animals and reports behavioral issues to St. Nicholas.

According to two Swiss friends I made at the school, there was a certain process that one must go through before being able to perform as St. Nicholas. While both men had fully met the stringent requirements, one had served in the role a few years longer than the other. Therefore, the less tenured St. Nicholas was relegated to the role of Schmutzli for the entirety of the three-day Santa school. Rumor around the class was that Schmutzli wasn't happy about playing second fiddle. Whether true or not, I'll never know.

Meeting with them and learning about their culture was a delight, despite the fact that Schmutzli appeared to be a bit testy.

Stories

As a writer, Santa school offered me a fountain of ideas. Early in 1998, I assembled scraps of notes and snapshots of discussions and wove them into a story. I sent "Helpers" to an acquaintance who worked for the retail clothier Lands' End. To my great delight, the short story was published in the October 1998 edition of the Lands' End Christmas catalogue. My name was listed, along with Garrison Keillor and Frances Mayes, as authors of feature articles.

I was flushed with pride. After years of failed submissions, I had finally managed to get an original piece published. The reality was overwhelming. For one reason or another, I was afraid to read it. When I finally read the story in the catalogue, I was convinced I hadn't actually written it. Only after I went back to a printout of my original story did I realize that I had, indeed, written the story titled "Helpers."

Helpers

A Short Story

The Helper trudged through blowing snow and growing drifts that Christmas Eve. Hands and tips of ears were numb from cold. In the middle of the woodlot between his farm and the neighbor's, he stopped to cut a small pine tree. The scrawny pine cradled under his arm, his free hand carried an old-fashioned railroad lantern. The wick on the oil lamp inside burned brightly, and the lantern cast red beams in four directions. The Helper's right hand was secured around the neck of a burlap sack that had been dyed a faded green.

Driving wind slapped his face, and snow stung his eyes and pierced his exposed skin like needles. The crest of the hill seemed to grow farther away while each step grew heavier. Breath came in heavy gulps. Despite the cold, the Helper could feel trickles of sweat beneath his handmade suit. Near the top, he stopped and pointed the lantern toward the sleepy farmhouse below. After a short break, he left the burning light at the crest of the hill and walked toward the house.

Inside, the poor farmer and his wife were tucking their children into bed after a final Christmas story. The family was saying its bedtime prayers when they heard a loud knock at the door. The children jumped out of their beds. Little feet didn't even feel the harsh cold of the linoleum floor and drafty staircase. The farmer and his wife had no idea what was happening, but their children did.

Outside their now opened door stood Santa Claus. At least the person standing in the doorway looked a bit like Santa to the children.

"Ho! Ho! Ho! Merry Christmas!" the Helper shouted at the top of his voice. The three older children cheered with delight, hopping up and down in place. The youngest still clung to his mother, unsure of what to make of the person at their door. Both the poor farmer and his wife were too shocked to speak.

"May I come in for a moment?" the Helper asked. "I would like to drop off a few gifts for the children."

"Why, yes ... please come in from the cold." The farmer opened the door wide and ushered the Helper inside.

The Helper slung the burlap sack over his shoulder, used the little pine tree as a cane, and walked into the house. Once he found the parlor, the Helper stood the little tree on end in a corner. The family gathered around him by the undecorated tree.

"Now," the Helper said, "who wants to sing some Christmas carols with me?"

The Helper sat on the floor and they joined him in singing all of their favorites: "Away in a Manger" to "Rudolph the Red-Nosed Reindeer." A warm spot glowed in the drafty old house as little bobs and bangles decorated the tiny tree.

After the singing, the Helper picked up his green bag. "I must leave you," he said. "This is my busiest night of the year. Before I go, though, I have gifts for each of you." The Helper adjusted his cotton beard before continuing. "Please, sit down."

The children sat cross-legged on the floor, bouncing in excitement. The poor farmer was spellbound. Mother was cautiously amused. The youngest child smiled. The kindness and spirit of the Helper and the surprise of his appearance ... was overwhelming. The parents just stood near their children and watched in wonder as the Helper reached into his sack.

The first gift was for Jeremiah, the oldest. The item had been rolled in crinkled brown paper, twisted at the ends, and wrapped in yellow ribbon tied in a bow. After the boy removed the ribbon, the Helper decorated the scrawny pine tree with it. The gift inside was a pocket knife with a bone handle and two blades. Jeremiah was so excited; he didn't notice that the knife wasn't new or that one of the blade tips was broken.

Naomi received a hairbrush. Mary was given a comb

and a hairpin. Benjamin, the youngest, received a hand-carved train engine.

The ribbons and paper wrappings were lovingly placed on branches, turning the spindly pine into one of the most beautiful Christmas trees ever.

Finally, the Helper reached deep into the sack and gave each child a peppermint candy and some new shoes that would last until spring.

As he turned to leave, the Helper handed his sack to the poor farmer. "You will find some bread and a few grocery items inside," he said, "and your neighbor will be stopping by tomorrow to share some of his coal for the winter." The poor farmer and his wife fought back tears and thanked him.

The family followed as the Helper walked toward the door. "Where are your reindeer?" the children asked. The chorus grew louder. "We want to see your reindeer," they pleaded as he opened the door.

The Helper turned and said, "My reindeer are very shy. If they see you, they will fly off. Then I won't be able to visit the other children tonight."

Shy Benjamin suddenly pulled away from his mother. "Please, Santa, can we just see your reindeer?"

"Well ..." the Helper said as he stroked his cotton beard, "maybe there is a way for you to see them. But you must promise to stay inside the house."

The Helper took them to a kitchen window that over-looked the snow-covered field. He extended his finger and pointed to the crest of the hill. "See that red light out there?" At first, they struggled to see the point of light standing out against the blizzard. Then, one after the other, they all saw it.

"That light, my friends, is coming from Rudolph's nose," the Helper said. "You children stay here and watch as I fly away on my sleigh."

With that, the Helper wished the family a Merry Christmas and walked out into the howling night. He pushed through the blizzard, protecting his eyes from the pelting snow. When he finally reached the hilltop and the lantern, he picked it up slowly and caught his breath for a moment. The Helper clearly saw the light from the farmhouse, but he could only imagine the children who were watching the pinpoint of red light in the midst of the snowstorm.

He gathered himself and took a few deep breaths before taking off downhill for the woodlot, holding the lantern high. Old muscles ached and screamed as he ran for all he was worth. The Helper stumbled in the deep snow but quickly regained his footing. As he neared the trees of the woodlot, he threw the railroad lantern high into the trees. The lamp struck a branch and went out instantly. The Helper collapsed onto the snow, exhausted. After a short rest, he picked himself up and walked slowly home, thankful for this opportunity to help.

To this day, those children remember the night Santa came to their house on Christmas Eve. Though they have long forgotten the simple gifts and candy, they clearly remember watching Rudolph, the other reindeer, and Santa flying from their field and into the dark of a snowy night.

First Night, Part One

The "suit" arrives. (1996)

Nearly twenty years ago, I put on the red suit for the first time. Looking at the pictures taken of me that night, I realize I was far too young and a bit too lean. And my makeup and beard were not quite up to par.

Regardless, I wanted to get some experience after graduating from Santa School. To get the ball rolling, I contacted a local preschool and volunteered to visit their Christmas production.

The school was delighted, and arrangements were made.

At the end of the program, as the children sang "Here Comes Santa Claus," I approached the stage. After greeting the students and the crowd, I led the children in singing "Rudolph the Red-Nosed Reindeer." Once the program was over, I was blessed with the opportunity to visit with the students and their families. As I sat near the entryway of the building in a large chair, a line of children quickly wound around the room several times.

Of all the children who filed through with their stories and quickly scribbled lists, one particular child remains in my warmest thoughts. A young girl kept coming through the line. She was about eight years old, bright-eyed and fair haired. Each time she came around, she requested the same gift and asked me a different question. *How do the reindeer fly? How do you know where I live? How do you get around the world in one night?*

She and her family stayed until the very end. I waited in the vestibule until they left the building and the janitor started turning off the lights. The last thing I wanted was for her to see Santa Claus riding off in a car.

That evening, there was an inch or so of new fallen snow. The fresh blanket sparkled like diamonds in the night. The little girl and her father walked hand in hand through the near-empty parking lot. My wife and I stood outside, waiting. We watched as the little girl let go of his hand and spun around to face me.

"I've got to know," she shouted. "Are you the *real* Santa Claus?"

With a friendly wave, I followed them through the snow-covered parking lot. As Dad buckled the little girl into the back of the family minivan, I poked my head inside the vehicle and she repeated the same question, "Are you the real Santa Claus?"

A day or two earlier my beloved wife had given me a pair of Christmas socks. They were blue with green lettering that proclaimed: "The Real Santa is Wearing These Socks." That night, in the glow of an overhead light inside a minivan, I removed my black boots and showed the little girl my socks. Her eyes grew wide as she read the words.

As I put my boot back on and walked away, I heard her whisper, "I just knew it!"

Dad slowly closed the door and secured it before turning to me. His words ring in my memory: "Thank you for giving me one more year of magic."

That experience with the curious little girl has a special place in my heart.

I could have never imagined that my first night would shape my future as a representative of a living legend. However, kind readers, that is the topic for First Night, Part Two.

First Night, Part Two

First night out the door. (1996)

On our way home from the preschool pageant, my wife was behind the wheel as usual. Our spirits were high as we recounted the moments of the evening, especially the story that we affectionately refer to as "The Sock Girl."

Our route home passed by the local fire department. I asked Deb to pull into their parking lot. An idea had formed in my mind. FYI, I have a true penchant for crazy ideas and my loving wife is generally game to indulge me.

Before leaving home that evening, I had grabbed a handful of candy canes and the wrapped lump of coal I'd gotten at Santa Claus School from Little Devin. Deb parked the car and we stepped into the wintry night and into the local fire department for an impromptu visit.

The dispatchers smiled when they saw us. Remember, I was still in the suit.

"Where are the firemen?" I asked.

One dispatcher grinned widely. "They're in a training meeting ... down the hall to the left. Take the first door on your right."

Without hesitation, Deb and I followed his directions. Before long, we burst through the doors of the meeting. The Chief was in the middle of a PowerPoint presentation. I interrupted as gracefully as possible.

First, I thanked the firefighters for their service and bravery while handing out candy canes to each of them. When I got around to addressing the chief, I gave him the green felt bag with its lump of coal and mumbled aloud about him being kind of a stinker lately.

The firemen broke out in huge guffaws and clapped their hands. Everyone enjoyed a good-spirited laugh. I wished them all a safe holiday season and made a quick exit, just like I had been taught at Santa school.

As my wife and I walked back to our four-wheeled sleigh, I heard the sound of footfalls behind us. When I spun around to get in the car, a young firefighter caught up with me. "Excuse me, sir," he began. "Chief wants to know if you'd like to help out with the city's Christmas tree lighting."

Of course, I said yes.

That first night at the preschool Christmas party and the local fire department set my life on a new and blessed path.

The Beard

Through the majority of my adult life, I
have sported facial hair, usually closely trimmed.
Several years before going to Santa School, I took
a job with a Fortune 100 company. During my
first annual performance review, my supervisor
noted, "If you want to go anywhere with the
company, you might want to consider shaving off
your beard."

Like a faithful idiot, I complied. During a
business trip to Peoria, Illinois, I purchased a razor

and watched my facial hair circle the drain. When I arrived home after being on the road, my family nearly revolted. My daughter broke down in tears when she first saw me. My wife and son didn't take it much better.

Fast forward a few years. I was still working for the corporation and still bald faced. Part of my job was to organize a national sales meeting to take place in Tucson, Arizona. Several hundred people would be gathering from all over the country at a resort in the hills outside of town. To help keep the mood light, I retained the services of two comedians, one of whom had a full beard. It was during a conversation with this funny man when my life changed for the good.

"I really like your beard," I said.

"Why don't you grow one?" was his response.

"Well, I had one for a while," I replied. "But my boss told me that if I wanted to go anywhere in the company, I should shave it off."

His response was profound. "Have you gone anywhere?"

From that day forward, I've always had a full beard and I've never looked back.

After volunteering to entertain the students at the Indiana School for the Blind, I decided to let my beard blossom during the year so it would be ready for the holiday season. Not all of the students who attend the Indiana School for the Blind are totally blind. Some have extreme tunnel vision; others have only peripheral vision; while others are not sightless at all, but have a condition that will in time cause them to be blind. Having a real beard for the students was important to me.

One day, I decided to make a fateful trip to my supervisor's office. Gene was a gruff looking, bulldog of a man. Betraying his outward appearance though was a thoughtful person with a strong mind and a big heart.

During our meeting, I played the only card I had: company policy. At the time of our discussion, the company had adopted a policy that encouraged diversity and celebrated differences between employees. "Gene," I began, "all I've been hearing about is how the company wants to embrace diversity. So, I plan on being your example of style diversity." I explained I would be growing a beard each year and why.

"Will it interfere with your job?" he asked.

"No," I replied.

Gene laughed. "Then I don't care what you do."

Surprisingly, once I started growing a full beard, I started going places with the company. Eventually, I worked myself into a position of great responsibility, often in contact with the top leaders. During that period, the CEO was an Aussie who, with his distinctive accent, often called me 'Santer.'

Getting it Right

When I started out, I was too young to be Santa. My beard and what was left of the hair on my head was fairly dark. (Time has magically taken care of that issue.) Along with my official red suit, I purchased a Yak hair wig and beard set. I wore the fake stuff for a short period of time, but it didn't suit me. Nor did it fool the children at the School for the Blind or any other place.

The trouble was: how to turn dark hair white?

The first attempt involved a greasy chalk material mixed with baby powder. Fail. It looked lumpy and chalky. The next attempt involved a trip to the beauty shop to have my hair dyed white. Double fail. Instead of turning my hair white, my hair and beard took on a brassy, copper color.

After years of experimentation and disappointment, the answer finally came to me: I would dye my hair and beard on my own with bleaching materials from a local beauty supply store. (I even had a discount card for a while.) I begin the bleaching process in late September or early October. It generally takes two to three treatments (at least a week apart) to get it right. Warning: the materials used in this process are toxic and dangerous. My advice is to rely on the skills and knowledge of professionals.

A Gift for Santa

I find the vast majority of children to be kind, loving, and generous· Many times, children will show what is in their hearts by giving gifts to Santa· These gifts are usually handmade and exhibit wonderful creativity· Each gift is precious and lovingly made·

The artwork I receive usually contains Christmas trees that are beautifully decorated·

Each year I see lots of wonderful stick figures,

odd-shaped heads, and lots of glue and glitter. Rudolph tends to be a favorite for many children. I also enjoy receiving hundreds of portraits of myself, some with cotton beards glued onto carefully drawn pictures.

One ice-cold evening as I was visiting children at Bay City's Santa House, a young boy came to see me. As he stood directly in front of me, he had a huge smile on his face and was hiding something behind his back. He handed me a gift—a red plastic cup with a hole cut in the bottom. A soda straw was sticking through the hole. Glued to the end of the straw was a hand-colored picture of me, Santa Claus.

I examined the cup and remarked on what a nice job he had done. I thanked him and turned to put the gift aside; however, before I could set it down, he stopped me.

"Do you know what it is?" his small voice squeaked.

I stroked my beard and scrunched up my face. "No," I admitted sheepishly. "I guess I don't know what it is."

He took the red plastic cup in one hand and pushed up on the straw with his other hand. The hand-colored picture of me popped up out of the cup.

"See," he said. "That's you coming up out of the chimney." Then he pulled down on the straw and the picture disappeared below the lip of the cup. "And that's you going down the chimney."

We laughed together and played with the exquisite gift. It was delightful. What a joy it was to see his excitement as he shared it with me. I still have that gift. I keep it in a special place in my office where I can see it (and play with it) whenever I want. Santa is just a big kid!

Help for Santa

One unseasonably warm December afternoon, I was at a Santa House downstate. Many children came to see me to share their Christmas wishes and dreams.

I distinctly remember one very special boy named Alex; who was neatly dressed in a white collared shirt, tie, and sweater. It was obvious he had carefully prepared for the visit.

Alex signed the guestbook in front of my chair using his best penmanship. As he carefully formed each letter of his name, his tongue stuck out of the corner of his mouth. Once finished, he fearlessly walked up to me and began to tell me how good he'd been all year. It was obvious he had rehearsed his speech.

We talked for a long time, discussing his school, his family, and his friends. He was an articulate and well-spoken young boy. Before long, I asked him if there was something special he wanted for Christmas.

Without hesitation, Alex said, "I want a red, radio-controlled car."

I thought about the request for a moment. "Do you want the battery-powered kind or the gas-powered kind?"

"I want the battery-powered kind!" Alex stated emphatically. "And I'd really like it to be red."

"Red's my favorite color too." I said. "Well, I can't promise that I'll bring you a red, radio-controlled car for Christmas. But if I do, you have to promise not to play with it in the house."

Looking up at me with wide, sincere eyes, Alex vowed not to play with an outside toy in the house. I wished him a Merry Christmas and gave him a peppermint candy. As he hopped off my lap and started to walk away, he suddenly turned and handed me a crumpled envelope. Since there was a long line of excited children waiting to talk with me, I told Alex I would read his note later, when I had a quiet moment. He politely said thank you and walked away.

Later that evening, as I was hanging up the suit, I found the envelope Alex had given me. I opened it carefully and extracted the contents. Alex had written me a letter on paper torn from a spiral notebook. The note was carefully written in the printing style of the early grades. It contained Alex's name and address. The body of the letter described all of the good things he had done during the year. Everything was in the same order and style of his rehearsed speech to me. Alex concluded with a reminder that he wanted a red, radio-controlled car for Christmas ... just in case I forgot.

The best part of the note was something I hadn't seen before or ever since. Taped to the bottom of the letter was a coupon good for $10 off on a radio-controlled car at Radio Shack. The car in the coupon was red, of course!

I can't help but smile whenever I remember Alex and his letter.

Kevin's Question

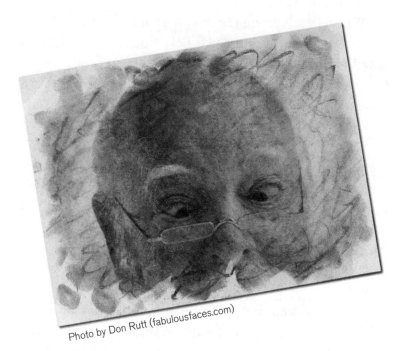

Photo by Don Rutt (fabulousfaces.com)

Kevin was eight years old and he was in the hospital with pneumonia just before Christmas. As I walked into his room, he was playing a video game. When he finally noticed me, he sat up straight and did a double take. His eyes opened wide and his jaw dropped.

Kevin put down his game controller and looked me up and down. "Hi, Santa," he said.

In short order, we were talking like old friends.

He showed me the IV tube that was in his arm, and he told me that it didn't hurt too much. I told him I was proud of how brave he was.

When we got around to talking about Christmas, Kevin told me that he wanted some new video games. Later, I asked him if he had any questions for me. He just shook his head no and shrugged his shoulders. "Are you sure?" I continued. When he didn't respond, I told him that I would look in on him before I left the hospital that night.

After leaving Kevin's room, I visited several other children. I was happy to find out that most of them would be going home for Christmas. Still, I told them that I wouldn't forget them on Christmas, no matter where they were.

After I completed my rounds, I stopped back to see my friend Kevin.

"Well," I began, "do you have any questions for me now?"

Kevin screwed up his face, like he was thinking really hard. Then he blurted out a question that I'd never considered. "Santa, who gave you toys when you were a little boy?"

I took a seat on the edge of his hospital bed. My mind raced for a good answer. "Kevin, I was the one who started to give toys to good children at Christmas. So, no one gave me toys when I was a little boy."

Kevin's face took on a scowl. Before he could say anything, I continued. "Don't be sad, Kevin, there is a lot more to Christmas than just presents and toys." He agreed. Then I continued, "Did you ever make something special for your mother, like a drawing or a craft at school?" The young man nodded in response. "Remember how good it made you feel to see your mom open her special present?" Again, Kevin nodded. "Well, I get that special feeling every Christmas. In fact, I think it is a lot more fun to give gifts than to receive them."

Before leaving, I shook Kevin's hand and gave him a warm smile. As I headed out of his room, I saw him reaching for the phone next to his bed. As I walked down the hospital corridor, I distinctly heard Kevin announce to the duty nurse: "I gotta call my mom about this!"

Suddenly Shy

For many years I arrived at our community tree-lighting ceremony on a shiny, red firetruck. The sirens blared and the horns blasted a wall of sound as the firemen drove me to the big Christmas tree that stood in front of the town hall. As I stepped down from the truck, a crowd of children gathered around me. It's always great fun to kick off the holiday season with these little ones. I handed out candy canes and small plastic Christmas rings from my green-velvet bag. Some rings had a snowman on them, others a Christmas tree.

One year, as I was talking to the children, I couldn't help but notice one tiny girl with golden locks. She had carefully woven her way to the front of the crowd. She was bundled in a green ski jacket and wore Big Bird mittens. They were bright yellow with eyes that rolled with each movement of her hand. When she finally got close to me, she just looked up and stared without saying a word.

I crouched down to her level and said, "Well, hello. How are you?"

Instantly, she spun around and ran straight to her father. She buried her little head between his knees and firmly hugged his legs. Her father gently picked her up and held her. He softly talked to her as he walked toward me. Goldilocks put her head down into the crook of his neck and refused to look at me.

"I don't understand," Daddy said. "All she's talked about was coming to see Santa Claus." He comforted her and tried his best to get her to tell me what she wanted for Christmas.

"That's all right," I said. "It's okay to be shy. Maybe you and your daddy can write a letter and tell me what you want."

Her father thought that was a good idea. She, however, remained silent. Her head stayed buried in Daddy's shoulder. As I was about to turn my attention to some other children, a thought occurred to me. I looked up at her father and asked, "Do you think she would like a special Christmas ring?"

He bounced his daughter lightly in his arms as he asked, "Would you like a ring?" She didn't make a peep; didn't turn her head. Instead, she slowly loosened her grip on his shoulder and dropped her left arm to her side. Then, a cupped hand inside its Big Bird mitten rotated toward me. All the while, her head remained embedded in her father's collarbone. I placed a Christmas tree ring in Big Bird's mouth and felt tiny fingers close around it.

"Merry Christmas, sweetheart," I said.

Without warning, that tiny child found a very big voice. "I want a toy kitchen … I want a doll that talks … I want … Once she got going, there was no stopping.

Assembly Not Included

Now and then, children freeze at the moment of truth. Their minds simply go blank. Sometimes they get so excited or nervous when they visit me, they can't remember a thing they want for Christmas. I call this condition "vapor lock."

One quiet afternoon, several weeks before Christmas, when the weather was unusually warm, a dad brought his daughter and younger son to see me.

The little brother talked a mile a minute, telling me in detail all the things he wanted for Christmas. His was a long and rambling list. The little guy jumped with excitement as he recounted his wishes. Unfortunately, big sister "vapor locked." When I asked her what she wanted for Christmas, all she could do was shrug her shoulders and say, "I can't remember." Disappointment was written on her face.

Because of the warm weather, traffic inside the Santa House was a bit slow that day; so I gave her plenty of time to think. Her father tried to help her remember, but she just couldn't. She wiggled and wriggled. She kicked her legs and thought real hard. But, nothing came.

Finally, she leaned back, looked up, and said, "I think I'd like a ceiling fan."

I followed the general direction of her glance and noticed that she was staring at the fan mounted high in the pitched ceiling above my Santa chair. "A ceiling fan," I repeated, doing my best to stifle a laugh. "Well, if I bring you a ceiling fan, I won't be able to install it for you."

"That's okay," her little brother piped up. "You didn't put together the playset you brought us last year either."

Ho! Ho! Ho! Little rascal.

Uncle Bud

*A short story, in loving memory of
Aunt Sophie and in honor of my cousins.*

Uncle Bud was always high-spirited. Some said he was downright goofy. Throughout his life, Uncle Bud constantly played tricks and jokes on family and friends. We never knew exactly what he was going to do—but we could always count on surprise and excitement whenever Uncle Bud was around.

One Halloween, he dressed up as a slimy sea monster and scared all the kids in the neighborhood. And there was the mongoose trick that lives on in family memory. When Aunt Sophie tripped the cage door, a stuffed animal shot out of the cage at her. She let loose with an ear-piercing scream and nearly jumped out of her skin. Everyone roared with laughter.

But all of the craziness was long ago. Uncle Bud, now in his eighties, has slowed considerably. However, whenever I see my favorite uncle, I remember the year I turned eleven like it was yesterday. It was the year I thought Uncle Bud was playing Santa Claus at the family Christmas party; and it is when I learned a life lesson about friendship and compassion.

Aunt Sophie arrived at the party at our house without Uncle Bud, which was unusual because they were always together. Aunt Sophie told everyone about what had happened earlier that afternoon. While shoveling snow, Uncle Bud had slipped on a patch of black ice in the driveway and broken his leg. Sophie told us that Bud had gone to the hospital and his leg was put in a plaster cast. "When I left home," she said, "he was doing just fine, but seems to be in a lot of pain. He's just resting in bed with his leg up on pillows." As Aunt Sophie removed her coat and hat, she made a point to say, "Bud sends his love to everyone."

No family Christmas party would be the same without good ol' Uncle Bud. His joy and enthusiasm was contagious. However, the powers of toy avarice are overwhelming. All of the cousins were excited that the Christmas season had finally arrived. Our house was filled with the glittering lights, comforting sounds, and delightful smells of the holiday. The sweet chaos of love and laughter floated in the air. Family swept through the buffet like a swarm of locusts; flimsy paper plates were laden with our favorite foods.

Mom played the piano and we all sang Christmas carols. Afterward, all of us kids got to open presents from our secret Santas. As the wrapping paper began to fly, we heard the doorbell ring. I remember the look on Dad's face as he crossed the living room to open the door. "Who could that be?" he mumbled as he twisted the doorknob.

Dad opened the door slightly and peeked outside. "My goodness!" he said. "Look who's here." He threw the door open wide and stood aside, shouting, "It's Santa Claus!"

There, in the doorway, stood the man himself. At least, he looked like Santa, dressed all in red and white. My younger brother and sister, along with our cousins, jumped with joy and clapped their hands in excitement. They squealed in delight as the jolly old elf joined in the celebration.

I, on the other hand, had a sneaking suspicion Santa was really Uncle Bud dressed up in the suit. While the other children gathered around him, I withdrew to a corner of the room. I was too old for this stuff. Uncle Bud couldn't fool me.

Dad calmed things down a bit and invited our guest to have a seat. Santa said he didn't have much time; but he was happy to visit with each of the children. While the others stood in line to talk with Santa, I held back.

Earlier that week, one of the guys at school had told me there was no such thing as Santa Claus. I didn't want to believe what he said, but almost everyone else in class agreed with him. It made me sad. That night at the family Christmas party, I was convinced my friend at school was right. Although the beard looked real, I was sure Uncle Bud was playing Santa.

Once all the kids were done with their visits, my mother turned to me. "Don't you want to tell Santa what you'd like for Christmas?"

I shook my head and quietly said, "No." A part of me wanted to say yes, but doubt held me back.

"Well then," Santa said, "I must be on my way. I've got a busy night ahead of me, that's for sure." He placed both hands on his knees and jumped up from his seat. Then

Santa walked around the living room to shake hands. I held back, feeling somewhat betrayed. As Santa stepped out into the snowy night, everyone else waved good-bye. As he left, I couldn't help but think that Uncle Bud would be showing up in a short time.

We all pitched in to pick up bright wrapping paper, boxes, and dirty plates. Afterward, Mom asked me to help the little ones get ready for bed. Once everything was in order, I put on the new pajamas I got from Aunt Dale. When I was halfway down the staircase, I heard the door-bell ring.

I took the stairs two at a time and threw open the door. As I suspected, there in the dim yellow porch light stood Uncle Bud. Rather than confirming my earlier hunch, my jaw dropped in shock. Long wooden crutches supported his body. His right leg was in a plaster cast from his knee to his foot. His exposed toes were black. Uncle Bud looked sore, tired, and in lots of pain.

"Merry Christmas, Charlie," Uncle Bud said weakly. "May I come in?" He winced as he carefully maneuvered the crutches and a badly injured leg in a heavy plaster cast. While holding the door open, a taxi backed out of the driveway and tooted its horn. The cab sped away, fishtailing down the street on a fresh layer of slippery snow.

Mom and Dad, along with all the aunts and uncles, raced into the living room to help Uncle Bud settle into a chair. Cousins gathered around and loved on our favorite uncle, while Aunt Sophie lifted his broken leg onto the ottoman. "Bud," she said in a scolding tone, "I told you to stay home and get some rest."

Uncle Bud gave his wife a sheepish look over the tops of his glasses. "Shoot, I couldn't miss all this fun. Besides, if my leg is going to hurt, it won't hurt any worse here than it will at home."

"All right, all right," Aunt Sophie said as she shuffled back to the kitchen. "I'll fix you something to eat." The little ones were sent to bed, and the adults returned to their raucous card game in the dining room. After Aunt Sophie brought a plate of warmed leftovers, I had my favorite uncle to myself.

"Uncle Bud," I asked tentatively, "how did you hurt your leg?"

"Didn't your Aunt Sophie tell you?" he replied between mouthfuls. "I was shoveling snow this afternoon when I slipped on some ice in the driveway and took a tumble." He took a sip of hot coffee before continuing. "When I tried to stand up, a terrible pain shot through my leg. Your Aunt Sophie took me to the hospital. Next thing I knew, some doctor was putting this on my leg." He knocked on the hard cast with his knuckles. "I'll be wearing it for at least six weeks."

"How come your toes look black?" I asked.

Uncle Bud winced in pain as he wiggled the black toes that stuck out of the bottom of the cast. "Sometimes when you break your leg, your toes turn black. My leg hurts like the dickens," he replied. "And it itches too."

I studied my uncle as he finished his food. In my mind, I checked off the differences between Santa and Uncle Bud. Santa seemed to be a bit taller, and he was a lot bigger around the middle. As I recollected, Santa's voice was deeper. Uncle Bud was clearly in pain and it was difficult for him to walk. On the other hand, Santa bounded around the room, full of energy.

As I weighed the evidence, I came to the unmistakable conclusion that Uncle Bud couldn't have been playing Santa Claus. My heart sunk. I had missed my chance to tell Santa what I wanted for Christmas. Staring straight ahead, a tear formed in the corner of my eye and tumbled down my cheek.

Uncle Bud squeezed my arm gently. "What's wrong, Charlie?"

"Uncle Bud," I began, "one of my friends at school told me that Santa isn't real." My uncle handed me a handkerchief, and I blew my nose. "Tonight, Santa came here to the family party. I thought he was you in a Santa suit. But, now I know it wasn't you."

Even though I was supposed to be a young man, I put my head on my uncle's shoulder and cried softly. I dearly loved Uncle Bud even back then, but I hadn't thought of him as a friend until that night. As I melted down, he stroked the back of my head and told me everything was going to be alright.

"You don't understand, Uncle Bud," I said, wiping my eyes with the sleeves of my new pajamas. "I didn't get to tell Santa what I wanted for Christmas. Now, while everybody else will be opening presents on Christmas morning, I'll be sitting there empty handed."

"It's okay," Uncle Bud reassured me kindly. He thought for a moment before continuing, "I think I know how to get a message to him. Go get a piece of paper and a pencil; we'll write him a note."

Charged with a new sense of hope, I ran upstairs and grabbed a sheet of paper and a pencil from my desk. Aunt Sophie was taking away the dirty dishes and refilling his coffee cup when I returned. "You boys doing alright?" she asked kindly. Uncle Bud and I nodded our response. "You need a pain pill, Bud?"

Uncle Bud gave me a hug and mussed my hair, "Na, I've got everything I need right here." As Aunt Sophie walked back to the kitchen, Uncle Bud took a big sip of coffee and gave me a wink. Then he told me to get to work writing a letter to Santa.

"What do I write?" I asked.

Uncle Bud wrinkled his chin in thought. "Write him a letter about believing. Tell him what you feel and what you'd like as a special Christmas present. But, you'd better hurry, there isn't much time."

My best efforts went into writing that letter. I poured my heart out about the importance of believing and the real meaning of Christmas. The rambling letter also included a request for a real chemistry set. I promised to be careful and clean up the mess. When I finished, Uncle Bud took the letter and read it carefully. Then, he asked for my pencil and wrote a short note at the bottom:

Santa:

Charlie is a fine young man. If you can, please leave him a chemistry set for Christmas. Also, leave it behind the Christmas tree so Charlie will know for sure that you are real.

Your friend,
Bud

Uncle Bud examined the note and folded it carefully before placing it in his shirt pocket. Then he called out to my aunt. "Come on, Sophie," he shouted. "We need to get going. There's some important business to be done." As Bud hobbled toward the front door, he turned and looked at me. "Don't worry about a thing," he said with a wink, "Santa is a good friend of mine."

As I look back on that night, I marvel at the lessons I learned ... about the power of love, belief, and the people in our lives. I discovered the value of listening to my heart rather than placing trust in the views and opinions of others. Most importantly, that night was a lesson in friendship, the kind of friendship that pays no attention to age or time.

Very early that next Christmas morning, a commotion from downstairs woke the family as my brother and sister discovered the bounty of gifts. I threw off my covers and raced down the staircase, bounding to the back of the tree. There, hidden behind piney boughs, was a chemistry set and a microscope adorned with a bright red ribbon and bow. Taped to the set was a handwritten note:

Charlie:
    Your Uncle Bud is right! You are a fine young man.
Sincerely,
Santa

Uncle Bud's spirit is still strong, but time has taken its toll. It takes more effort to help him get around than it did that year his leg was broken. Even so, the extra effort is worth it.

This year, it was our turn to host the family Christmas party. At the end of the night, Aunt Sophie asked me to help Bud to the car. Walking through the crisp December snow together, he watched me closely through clouded eyes and thick glasses. His smile was still warm and comforting. Despite crippling arthritis and the aches of old age, he is still active. Uncle Bud leans hard against me with each step. I am thankful to be strong for him, just like he was strong for me so many years ago.

As I buckled him in the seat and began folding his walker to put it in the trunk of his car, uncle Bud waved me to his side and whispered. "There's something for you in the trunk." He patted me gently on the hand. "Open it once you get inside."

I retrieved an old army duffle bag from the trunk and placed the walker inside. Aunt Sophie backed the car out of the driveway and honked the horn as she drove away. When the taillights of their car faded into the night, I went back inside to take a look at the contents of the duffle bag.

With our children already tucked safely in bed, my beautiful wife was collapsed in her favorite chair. I brought the duffle into the living room and plopped it down onto the floor in front of the fireplace. "What's that?" she asked as I set about opening the bag.

"I don't have any idea. Uncle Bud told me to open it once I got inside."

"So," my wife said, "why don't you open it?"

Leaning down and pulling on the heavy zipper, the bag fell away to reveal some unusual items. My name was scratched across the face of an envelope that sat on the very top of the collection. The strangest of the items was a leg cast that was split down the middle and hinged at the back. Next was a folded set of wooden crutches. The bag also contained a small container of plaster and a can of black shoe polish.

The note inside the envelope was short and sweet:

It is a gift to help others enjoy the wonder of belief.
Love,
Uncle Bud

Remembrance

Santa and firefighters have a special bond.
It may be because these brave men and women
also spend a lot of time on rooftops; although I
suspect the reason is something else.

Every year on the Saturday before Christmas,
a group of firefighters I know, along with the
American Red Cross, visit the homes of needy
families. These thoughtful individuals let me travel
along with them in their big, shiny firetruck. Over
the years, we oftentimes visited with the same
families.

My job on these special outings was to
entertain and distract the children while the
firefighters hauled bags of groceries, toys, and
other gifts into the home. After I listened to the
kids' Christmas dreams and wishes, a helper would
take a Polaroid picture of me with each child. The
photo was then presented to the family.

These visits were always bittersweet. While
it is difficult to see families struggling, it is
heartwarming to share the spirit of Christmas and
see the sparkling little eyes filled with excitement.

On one such visit, we stopped at a home that was way out in the country. Both parents had been suffering with difficult and long-lasting health problems. It was obvious this family was having a very hard time making ends meet. There were two children. The oldest daughter had a full face, dark hair, and a warm smile. The youngest was shy and quiet.

As I began to talk with them, the oldest spoke up. "I remember you from last year."

"You do?" I responded. "Do you remember the gifts I left for you?"

The young lady tapped her finger on the side of her head as she thought. "Uh-huh. I think you brought me some clothes and some toys." Then her eyes brightened. "Wait right here, I remember something that you left for me last year."

She scurried out of the room. You could hear her footfalls as she raced through the house. Moments later she returned. In her hand she held the Polaroid picture that had been taken of us the year before. The picture was worn and wrinkled from much handling. We looked at the picture together, and I remarked how big she had gotten since the previous year.

This photo also gave me a glimpse of what our team's visit to this household had meant. Christmas was so much more than gifts and glitter. This moment was proof of that fact.

After the firefighters were done with their tasks, another Polaroid was taken of the two of us. That year, I held her just a little more closely.

The Princess

It was a cold, snowy afternoon when I traveled with the fire department, Red Cross volunteers, and Social Services personnel over dirt roads in the countryside. Eventually, we pulled into a long driveway and parked the vehicles between the house and barn. The two-story farmhouse stood stark against the grey clouds of late December. Its faded siding begged for a coat of paint and the windows covered in plastic shook in the wind.

During the journey from town, I learned that the man of the house had abandoned his family a few weeks before Christmas, leaving a young wife and daughter to fend for themselves.

As usual, my job was to go inside first. The firefighters, with their bags of clothes, food, and Christmas gifts, waited behind the firetruck for the signal to go to work once I had captured the attention of the child.

I was greeted in the small kitchen by a grateful mother who appeared to be carrying the weight of the world on her shoulders. "She's been waiting in the parlor for you all morning," she said in a hushed whisper as she pointed the way.

I passed through the kitchen and made my way to the parlor. The room was open and drafty. There, on a round table in the middle of the room, was a sparse Christmas tree decorated with big, colored lights; dripping with tinsel; and dotted with colorful bulbs. I scanned the entire room before I finally spotted a girl to my right.

She stood at the edge of a threadbare carpet. Her dress was worn, likely handed down, and obviously a few sizes too small. Faded colors exposed patterns of fairies and princesses. Long, thin arms picked at the edges of her dress and she curtsied.

I don't always know what I'm going to do from one minute to the next. For some reason, I dropped to one knee and opened my arms to that little girl.

"You look just like a princess," I said, with a voice that came from my heart.

She did a quick twirl and ran to me. Her hug is one I will remember for as long as I am alive. The skin on her arms was dry and cracked; her young life was upside down. But, for at least a moment, she knew she was very special.

Every year I put on the suit I think of that little princess.

A Joyful Noise

Photo by Don Rutt (fabulousfaces.com)

Each year, I am blessed to visit an indoor
family resort that offers activities for children
of all ages· It was a crisp, clear, and starry
December night at the resort when a girl and her
little brother approached my chair· As I visited
with big sister, I heard sounds coming from her
brother· He was all bundled up with a heavy coat;
a stocking cap pulled down over his ears; and a
thick, wool scarf around his neck· His outfit gave
him the appearance of a six-year old Michelin Man·

"Is he saying something?" I asked.

"No," she replied. "He's singing."

When I concentrated on his tiny voice, I started to make out the strains of "Rudolph the Red-Nosed Reindeer."

There is nothing more beautiful than a child's voice in song. Since the movie Frozen was released, I've asked hundreds of little girls to sing "Let it Go" from the movie. Surprisingly, twenty or so girls sing at least a portion of the song to me every year. (I keep an annual count.) Tonight was the first time a child had walked up to me singing "Rudolph."

"Do you want to sing Rudolph together?" I asked.

He nodded in excitement. The three of us sang like we were the only people in the world. Little brother particularly enjoyed singing the descants.

"Rudolph the red-nosed reindeer had a very shiny nose ..."

"Like a lightbulb," he intoned.

Soon, others in line sang along. The lights twinkled brighter, bulbs shined clearer, and the decorations were cheerier; making a wonderful Christmas memory for everyone.

Nate and Mary Ida

Nate Doan and Mary Ida Doan are two of the greatest names in the history of the legend of St. Nicholas. They were the only Santa and Mrs. Claus I knew as a child. Likewise, my children enjoyed annual visits with this amazing couple as well. Years later, when I attended Santa School, I discovered Nate and Mary Ida Doan were regulars. In fact, they ran the school between 1957 and 1971. Of the many stories they shared with me, the following one is my favorite.

Grand Theft Auto

    Nate worked in the local school system and spent his free time in the role of Santa. He never wanted to disappoint a child, and Nate prided himself at being punctual for his events. As it happened, one day he got caught up in his work and lost track of the time. When he realized he was running late, Nate panicked, threw on his winter coat, and raced out the door.
    He pressed the speed limit through town and raced into his own driveway. Nate threw the car

in park and ran inside. He was in such a hurry, he left the car running and the driver's door open. After a quick change into his suit and beard, Santa emerged from the back of the Doan house, jumped in the car, and peeled off down the street.

As always, Santa arrived right on time. Children, adults, and Santa himself enjoyed a delightful party. Afterward, Nate drove home, sneaking in the back door to make sure no one saw him. As he removed his beard and wig, the phone in the kitchen started to ring.

"Hello," he said.

"Nate, this is Mrs. Jackson from across the street," his neighbor began. "You won't believe what my son told me tonight."

Nate's curiosity shifted into high gear. "Really? What's that?"

"When I got home from work, my son ran up to me. Eyes wide, he was bubbling with excitement," she said. "When I asked him what was going on, he blurted out, 'Mom, you won't believe it! Santa Claus stole Mr. Doan's car. I saw it myself!'"

Joey

When I am in the chair, my attention is focused on the individual directly in front of me. Because of this, I am frequently surprised by the next person or family that steps forward.

One of my most pleasant surprises happened one winter night when I was at the Midland Santa House.

After I said good-bye to a young family, a small group stepped forward. Three adults, two women and one man, stood in front of me. The woman in the middle spoke for the group.

"Hi, Santa," she said. "My name is Mandy. I'm the caregiver for Amy and Joey." The adults at her side had the outward signs of Down Syndrome. Amy had a beautiful, round face that was split by the biggest smile I'd ever seen. Joey was her opposite. As he stood in front of me, it was easy to read that he carried a dour, embarrassed look of unbelief.

The caregiver noticed Joey's body language. "Santa," she said, "Joey thinks you're not real because you don't know his name."

The people inside the Santa House crowded in tightly to listen in on how this conversation was going to develop.

"What?" I asked. A smile spread across my face as I looked around. "Everybody knows that Santa loves Joey." I pointed at one of my helpers and said, "You know I talk about my friend Joey all the time, don't you?"

The elf agreed wholeheartedly. "Oh yeah, you and I were talking about Joey just a few minutes ago."

The crowd inside the house pitched in with comments. "Sure, Santa," one father joined in. "I've heard you mention Joey a time or two."

And from that moment forward, the people around us, young and old, eagerly became participants in the joyful conversation.

The candle was lit. Joey's face turned from gloom to sparkling joy. His whole perspective turned. And that is when we enjoyed a wonderful conversation about his job and his behavior. He told me that he'd been very good that year. Mandy, the caregiver, agreed and shared stories about how our friend Joey had been extra helpful. When I finally got around to asking what he'd like for Christmas, Joey told me that he wanted some walkie-talkies.

"So," I began, "you'd like a pair of two-way radios for Christmas?" Joey nodded enthusiastically. "What would you do with them if I brought you some?"

Joey scratched his chin as he thought about his answer. "I could be at the far end of the fence with one of the walkie-talkies and you could be by the road with the other ..." His imagination was running in full gear, and his face brightened. "We could talk to each other on the radio!" He exclaimed. Joey got so excited, he started to shake.

"What a great idea!" I said. Then I pointed to a grandfatherly man who was listening. "I'll bet you'd like to talk with Joey on the radio sometime."

The man's eyes grew wide. "That sure sounds like fun, Santa," he agreed.

I told Joey that I couldn't promise him a set of walkie-talkies for Christmas, but I'd do my very best. Then I turned the course of our conversation. Leaning into Joey's space, I asked, "Is Amy your girlfriend?"

Joey blushed. "Yes, she is."

Amy gushed. Her face glowed and her smile was so wide it stretched her eyelids into joyful grins. She told me that Joey was her boyfriend, and the two of them worked together nearly every day. When I asked her what she wanted for Christmas, her request was sweet and simple: a doll.

After we finished our chat, I reminded them about

being kind to each other and treating each other with respect. They promised they would.

As I recall, that particular night was a long one. Once the trains and sound system were shut down and the banks of lights extinguished, I fumbled in the dark and prepared myself for the drive home.

Santa always carries a flashlight—I tell children it's for dental inspections—but it comes in handy for other things. That night, the beam landed on the guest registry near the back door. The kind comments were heartwarming. And, as I turned the page to read more, what I saw shocked me to the core. Written across two full pages of the registry were the words:

Joey Loves Santa

Tattoos

    I live in small-town middle America where family togetherness is a hallmark. One of the benefits of living here is the support and kindness I get from my cousins.

    My cousin Harry runs a thriving tattoo shop. One day I mentioned to him my need for a few simple tattoos. Harry agreed to help me and offered the "family discount." I shared my ideas and told him I had the artwork.

    Harry said, "No problem." And we set a date.

The artwork for one of my two tattoos is a noble reindeer with a red nose. Underneath the reindeer are the letters SC. I tell people it is not the postal code for South Carolina. And, in the event that little ones, or big ones, can't readily translate the two letters under the red-nosed reindeer, my other arm spells it out: Santa Claus.

On my way home after getting my first tat, I picked up some antibiotic ointment and a six pack of barley-based beverages. It is important for you to know that, except for Harry, I'd discussed my plans to get a tattoo with no one—not even my wife.

When my beloved arrived home later that evening after a meeting, several items in the kitchen caught her attention. A small, white receipt was curled up on the dark countertop. The items on the receipt—antibiotic ointment and barley-based beverages—raised immediate suspicion.

The look on her face when she opened the bedroom door, turned on the lights, and waved the receipt in the air was classic. But let me back up a bit …

Prior to her arrival, I purposely placed the receipt on the counter so she'd notice it when she walked in. Then, I waited until I heard the garage doors open. I was wearing a pair of cargo shorts. Above the waist I wore nothing but antibiotic ointment and a thin layer of gauze over my new body art. I turned out the lights and covered myself with a sheet.

Back to her reaction …

She waved the receipt in her right hand and asked, "What's this?"

I pulled the sheet off my shoulder and lifted the gauze to expose my ink. Her mind whirled and engaged quickly. She stood at the foot of our bed and laughed at me. Not just ha-ha but the kind of laugh that makes your sides ache for days.

That moment embodies an important aspect of our marriage: that of unconditional love mixed with the enjoyment of playful surprise. Keeping life interesting and lively are vital aspects of happiness and longevity.

The body art has led to several interesting stories.

The Yard Sale

One summer day I was helping my daughter and son-in-law with a yard sale. I was inside the house working on something or other, unaware of a conversation that was taking place on the driveway.

Among the shoppers that day were a mother and her five-year old daughter. The sale merchandise or general exchange of ideas somehow drifted to the question of Santa Claus. The little girl stated her opinion that she didn't believe the real one ever visited the Santa House in town. To cap her comments, she stated that she knew the real Santa had a tattoo.

My wife happened to overhear their discussion. She turned to our granddaughter and said, "Go get Santa."

Natalie turned and burst through the house announcing, "Santa, you're needed outside, pronto!"

When I was outside, I was directed to the garage, where the girl and her mother were looking at yard sale treasures. When I walked up, the child turned and looked at me in shock. You see, I just can't get away from looking like "the man" most of the year; even at garage sales. I said to the young lady, "I heard you said that the REAL Santa has a tattoo."

She nodded boldly.

That's when I rolled up my sleeve and showed her my ink.

The little girl took a half step back and said one word, "Whoa."

Mother and daughter left the yard sale with big smiles, and a story for daddy.

On the Water

Like most people, I enjoy water sports in the summertime. One of my favorite activities is kayaking and boating in nearby lakes and rivers. It was a beautiful summer day and I'd just enjoyed an outing on a pristine lake. I was loading my kayak onto a trailer when I heard a small person yelling in his outside voice.

"Look, Dad! There's Santa Claus!"

The father tried to steer him away from me, apologizing for his child's behavior. My wife assured the man that everything was just fine and that this kind of thing happens all the time.

I called the father and son over to me and put a hand on the sleeve of my T-shirt, the sleeve that covers the SC tattoo. I pulled up the sleeve and exposed my reindeer tattoo. The young man was in awe and his father had a good laugh. That little boy walked away with a lifetime memory that only took a few seconds to deliver.

Dining Out

I never know when I'll encounter the look—a lingering stare from smiling eyes. It can come from the more mature as well as the young. The look is also sometimes intermixed with muttered conversations and finger pointing.

Generally, I acknowledge the opportunity and inevitably little ones approach and ask me if I am Santa. When possible, I give them as much time as they want. While I don't actually admit to being Santa, I'll flash the tattoo. That tends to satisfy their curiosity.

Christmas with Sister

A Short Story

"**Maggie! Sarah!** Hurry up now! It's time for bed."
Father called up the staircase. "You've got to be asleep or
Santa won't come."

We hurried into our pajamas and popped into our
toasty beds. Our parents came into our rooms and said
prayers with us before they trundled off to their own room
for the night. The excitement was so intense, we never
thought we'd fall asleep.

That Christmas Eve was cold and windy. A full moon
hung just above the leafless trees, and the breeze pushed
snow into small drifts at the foot of the house. The night was
alive with sounds. Branches swayed and clacked together.
Our old house creaked and groaned.

Time passed slowly. I tossed and turned. My heart
jumped at every noise. Staring out the window from the
warmth of my bed, I searched for signs of movement in the
dark. Suddenly, I saw a haunting reflection in the glass. My
breath caught in my throat and before I could scream, a
soft hand covered my mouth. "Sh-h-h-h!" Maggie kept her

voice low and calm. "Move over," she said. "Let's wait up for Santa together."

"What do you mean?" I asked as I slid to the far side of the bed.

"I can't sleep. So, I thought if you aren't sleepy, we could stay up through the night together. We might even be able to see Santa."

We snuggled together under a pile of warm blankets. As we lay together, a plan was hatched. On the landing halfway down the stairs you can see a clear reflection of our Christmas tree in the big front window. We would sneak to that exact spot and watch for Santa once we heard his sleigh on the roof.

My sister and I whispered stories and stuffed pillows in our faces when we laughed. I have no idea how long we stayed up. But, after a while, we both drifted into dreamland.

Sometime in the night, a loud creaking sound startled me awake. "Sarah," I whispered as I shook my big sister. "Do you hear that? I think it's Santa!"

She stretched her arms and arched her back into the bed. Suddenly, another sound came from downstairs. We gasped in unison and sat up, instantly awake and alert.

Ever so slowly, we kicked off the covers and eased out of my bed. The feet of our pajamas made soft flapping sounds as we shuffled across the carpet. As Sarah opened my bedroom door, its hinges squeaked and groaned. When the door started closing by itself, I took a teddy bear from the top of my dresser and used it for a doorstop. Together, we tiptoed onto the rug in the hallway.

Sarah stopped near the stairs and held up her hand, cupping it behind her ear. Our hearts were pounding as we stopped to listen. We heard another sound, this time louder and more pronounced than before. It was definitely coming from near the Christmas tree. Sarah hugged me tightly. Both of us were shaking with excitement. It was all we could do to keep from giggling out loud.

The noise level seemed to intensify as we drew near the staircase. Quietly, Sarah leaned over the railing, trying to get a look at what was going on downstairs. My sister put her arm around me and whispered in my ear, "You go first." I shook my head no, but she pushed me into the lead. My steps made muffled crunching sounds.

Inch by inch and moment by moment, the downstairs window came into view. Although I was in the lead, Sarah was so close behind that I could feel her breath on my neck. When we finally made it to the landing, we grabbed the handrail and slowly sat on the steps.

From between the wooden slats, we scanned the reflection of Christmas in our living room window. The shapes and shadows were unclear. Still, it was easy to tell that there were lots and lots of presents. As we moved closer to take a better look, a loud rattling noise came from the room. The tree shook violently and shiny bulbs rattled while the tinsel shook. Sarah pointed and whispered too loudly, "Look, it's Santa."

Both of us spun around and ran up the stairs as fast as our feet could fly. We tore into my room and jumped into bed at the same time. When we did, our heads bumped together with a loud cracking sound. I wanted to cry, but I was too scared. We threw the blankets over our heads and breathed heavily. Hearts thumped wildly as we rubbed the pain from our noggins.

"Do you think he saw us?" I gasped.

"I don't know," Sarah answered. "Maybe. For sure he heard us."

"What if he did?" I asked.

Sarah was quiet for a moment. "Father said that Santa wouldn't come if we were awake." In the darkness, I could only see the outline of my sister's face, but I could plainly hear the concern in her voice. "I sure hope he doesn't take our presents away."

The thought of Christmas without presents gnawed at us. We lay side by side through the long night, wide awake and staring at the ceiling. Both of us were too afraid to make a noise or move a muscle. Moments seemed like hours. Finally, long after sunrise, a stirring came from downstairs. Still, we waited quietly. Before long, the delightful smell of bacon sizzling on the stove rose up the staircase. Mother called out, "Merry Christmas! Maggie! Sarah! Come quickly!"

I looked at Sarah. She looked back at me. Each of us knew what the other was thinking. Santa had seen us. The moment had arrived. We would finally find out whether or not our presents had been taken back to the North Pole.

Slowly we eased out of bed. Holding hands and crossing fingers, we trudged down the same hallway we'd visited the night before. On the landing, we both stopped to peek at the front window. It didn't work like a mirror as it did during the night. Slowly, we eased around the bannister and peeked into the living room.

Boxes wrapped in green, red, and gold spilled out from under the Christmas tree. We stared in silent rapture for a moment before scrambling down the steps, squealing with joy. Our excitement was cut short when a large box started rattling and shaking, making a loud racket and shaking the Christmas tree. The closer we got to the box, the more noise it made.

We carefully approached the box; Sarah on one side and I on the other. Slowly, we lifted the top off the box to reveal the most wonderful present of all time. It was a St. Bernard puppy! Instantly, we realized we hadn't seen Santa after all. It was just our new puppy!

Our breakfast went cold and uneaten as Sarah and I nuzzled the dog. Right then and there we decided to name him Saint Nicholas, but we call him Nick for short.

After a time, Father came out of the kitchen to join us. He raised his coffee cup at us before taking a sip. "Did I hear you two monkeys get up in the middle of the night?"

Neither of us answered. We just covered our smiles and giggles with our hands. It's our special secret, so don't tell anybody.

Human Biology

Of the few questions I get from adults, many of them are centered around human biology. Whether it's news reporters, the curious, or whomever, the subject seems to gravitate toward the ultimate question: Has a child ever wet on you?"

The question completely misses the point about the wonder of a child's belief. Certainly, I've had children wet on me. Every year I get up close and personal with little ones with loaded diapers. I have also had children with life-threatening illnesses drool on me. I've closely hugged young and old people who were near death. Blind children have taken guided tours of my face, my beard, and the mosquito landing strip on the top of my head. A young man with Down Syndrome, total blindness, and acute hearing loss sat on my lap and told me he wanted a Braille calendar for Christmas.

In some of my happiest moments, I have signed "Santa loves you" to deaf children. I've been group-hugged by a classroom of handicapped little ones. Mentally impaired adults much larger than I am have occupied space on my lap and have shared their Christmas wishes with me. I've been kissed by old women with no hair and have shaken the bony hands of old men. Being Santa Claus means loving everyone equally and without hesitation—regardless of race, age, status, color, belief, body odor, or appearance.

It does, however, come with certain health risks.

Through the season, I get tired and my body weakens. This makes me susceptible to illness. I have spent five of the last twenty Christmases in an Emergency Room. One Christmas season, two sisters visited with me. At the end of our time together, one proudly announced that they had chicken pox. That holiday season, I spent Christmas Day in the hospital suffering with shingles.

Lots of kids with runny noses and hacking coughs talk with me each year. In recent years, I have started to wear white gloves. Thanks to the constant urging of my loving wife, I am healthier these days than ever before.

I am by no means perfect and have my own shortcomings. However, I believe that if each of us were to reach out just a little more to others in this world, it would truly be a better and more peaceful place.

Now, back to the diary ...

A Personal Question

It was a cold night, early in the Christmas season· After a few mild days, the thermometer had quickly dropped to near zero· The people in Midland, Michigan, were snuggled in against the extreme temperature· Not many families were visiting Santa's House·

During the lull, I got up from the big chair and walked around· There was plenty of imaginative craftsmanship to admire inside the building· As I examined the multiple sets of electric trains, a mother and her young son burst through the door, quickly closing it against the shattering cold· Both were totally bundled in cold-weather gear: thick, black coats; thick, wool scarves; heavy gloves; and heavy, wool stocking caps (toboggans for my Canadian friends)· They shivered and stomped to fight off the chill from the arctic blast·

I greeted them and welcomed them inside· They remained bundled as we walked through the house and talked· Mom took lots of pictures of her son and me in the big chair, in front of the animated elves, and at various other places inside the house. At the end of their visit, as they walked toward the door, I asked if the boy had any questions he'd like to ask me before he left.

The boy leaned toward me and slightly tilted his head. "Do you mind if I ask you a personal question?"

After many years of answering questions, this was a first. No one had ever begun a conversation in that manner. I was intrigued; so I said, "No, I don't mind. Please, ask me whatever you'd like." The boy's mother looked puzzled.

He pulled his hands out of his pockets and shrugged as he said, "Do you go to the bathroom?"

The mother's look quickly transitioned from puzzlement to embarrassment. Her bright smile instantly faded and she looked shocked.

I must admit I was taken aback as well. However, believing that honesty is truly the best policy, I answered, "Why, yes, I do. I'm just like everybody else, just a bit older."

The boy nodded as he absorbed my answer. Then he continued with his line of questioning. "Do you ever use other people's bathrooms?"

In the background, his mother was struggling to take his arm to escort him out of the Santa House.

I had an idea of where his questions were headed; so I answered. "Yes, I use other people's bathrooms from time to time."

"Have you ever used *my* bathroom?"

In answer, I gave the young man what can only be described as the "Santa Stink Eye," because it rolled through my mind that this kid might by trying to hang something on me. "I can't recall if I have used your bathroom," I responded. "However," I added, "it is important you clean up after yourself. And, always be sure to flush."

The mortified mother quickly marched her son out the door and back into the frigid night.

For the record, I have not had that particular question before or since—but I am ready for it.

Do Not Bring Presents

I receive lots of delightful letters from children· They are priceless in terms of their imagination and wonder· Many contain drawings of Santa and his reindeer· Some are lopsided stick figures (my favorites) and others are creative works of art·

Most of these young scribes ask for specific things· It is not unusual for children to cut pictures out of catalogues and paste them on their list. I have even had children bring entire toy catalogues with nearly every item marked. And there are letters that contain requests for others.

I also get many notes of heartwarming thanks and questions about my well-being. Many of these are striking and memorable. One, however, was especially poignant.

I remember her as though it happened just moments ago. She had blonde hair in tight curls that burst out of a knit cap. Her purple, insulated coat fell to her knees, and purple mittens covered her hands. Without saying a word, she extended her mittened hand. Her face was in a serious set and she seemed to be focused. There, in the crease between her thumb and her palm, was a folded piece of paper. I took the note from her, put on my reading glasses, and opened it. In the writing of a small child, the note read:

Dear Santa:
Do not bring presents for Clofur.
Clofur opens other peoples' presents.

I have had requests for all sorts of things over the years—from snakes to houses. Until reading this note, I'd never had a request to NOT bring presents to someone. Additionally, I was thinking that the name Clofur was unusual. However, different names and spellings are all too common in my line of work.

I looked at the little girl. "So, you don't want me to bring anything to Clofur this Christmas?" I asked. She nodded her head in agreement. "Has Clofur been bad?" I continued. Once again, she nodded her head. "Well, what did Clofur do that was so bad?"

The little girl was very serious as she told her story. "Last Christmas, Clofur woke up before everybody else." A look of exasperation was written on her face. This issue was genuinely troubling to her. "Clofur went to the Christmas tree and opened up everybody's presents. It was a big mess."

It was easy to see she was upset by Clofur's behavior. I looked around and did not see a brother or sister. After a pause to consider the matter, her mother recognized my puzzlement.

"Clofur is her cat."

"Well-l-l ..." My eyes widened as I thought about the horror of that moment when she saw her presents ripped to pieces. "I'll be sure to have a little talk with Clofur. Perhaps there is something you could do to keep Clofur away from the tree on Christmas Eve?"

She and her mother agreed it was a good idea. Who knew a cat could be so devious?

A Gift for Little D

One afternoon, when I was in my office (at my "real" job), a dear friend and coworker asked if I had a minute to talk. "Of course," I said. "Come on in."

She told me that her family would be visiting Santa Claus (me) that evening, and her children, William and Olivia, were really looking forward to it. She also shared that Olivia was taking horseback riding lessons. Her daughter absolutely loved riding her horse Little D. This nugget of information was priceless.

> *One of the joys in my life is to get inside information on the children I meet. For example, learning the names of their pets, their grade level in school, their teachers' names, any sports they enjoy, and other favorite things. Knowing these details helps their visit with Santa take on an added dimension of surprise. It makes our time together more magical and special. To see their eyes grow wide in amazement with the realization that Santa knows something about their lives adds to the wonderment—and is great fun for me, too!*

I was fully dressed in my Santa gear that evening when I stopped at the grocery store to pick up a bunch of carrots, some ribbon, and a small card.

Imagine seeing Santa Claus buying produce at a large grocery store! I received plenty of sideways glances from adults and ogling from children. But, nobody said a word to me.

Once I was in my car, I tied the ribbon around the bunch of carrots and on the card I wrote: "To Little D from Rudolph."

I could barely contain myself as I waited to see my friend and her children. About halfway through the evening, they showed up as promised. William and Olivia were dressed in their Christmas finest. Their excitement was contagious. We had a wonderful time together, talking about family traditions and special wishes, the stuff of life that makes the season so special.

As the family started to walk away, I stopped them in their tracks. "Olivia, wait!" I said. "Do you know a horse named Little D?"

Olivia spun around in surprise. She nodded her head yes, amazed by the fact that I knew the name of her real-live horse. While Olivia climbed the staircase to come back to me, I reached behind my chair and produced the carrots. I said, "I almost forgot. Rudolph asked me to give these to you in case I saw you tonight. They are a gift for Little D."

Olivia could not contain herself and started jumping up and down. What a delightful sight.

Everyone, including the people waiting in line, stopped their chatter to watch as the power of a special gift unfolded in front of them.

The next day, Olivia's mother couldn't wait to see me. She bubbled with excitement as she recounted the story of their ride home. Olivia talked incessantly about how Rudolph and Little D were the best of friends. She even came up with a very involved story about the time when Little D was going to horse summer camp and Rudolph was going to a nearby reindeer summer camp and they met over the fence.

Olivia's imagination blossomed. According to her, the two camps were right next to each other; Rudolph and Little D saw each other over the fence that separated the two camps. Both approached the fence and they began to talk. At once, they became the best of friends. That's why Rudolph gave Little D a gift for Christmas.

I just smiled and said, "That is *exactly* how they met."

Bad Handwriting

It was early in the evening, and there weren't many people in line waiting to see Santa, when a slender boy in a hoodie walked up to me· It is unusual for a child in a dark hoodie, drawn low on his face, to visit Santa· Without saying a word, he handed me a small piece of paper about half the size of a postcard· It was his Christmas list· He had each item listed from 1 to 5·

I often have to help children manage their expectations· I like it when they give me a list of just a few items, and I was pleased his list appeared to be manageable· Then I took to reading it, which is when things went crazy·

His penmanship was sloppy and illegible; so, I took out my magnifying glass to study the first item carefully before I spoke· (I keep a magnifying glass in my vest for teeth and ear checks·) His handwriting was a mess· Even with the magnifying glass, it was difficult to decipher·

When I recognized a set of letters as a word, I thought it was strange· I've had some unusual requests during my stretch in the chair; so I never question a wish· After some thought, I stooped low to catch his eyes before speaking·

"You want a toilet for Christmas?" I asked.

The young man was too stunned to speak. He took a step back, like he'd been hit by lightning.

"Ah," I said as I thought aloud, "maybe you want to be a plumber when you get older? I can't promise you a toilet for Christmas, but I'll do my best."

"No, Santa, no!" the boy appealed once the shock wore off. "I don't want a *toilet* for Christmas. I want a *tablet*. You know, like a small computer?"

Okay. The hieroglyph on the paper could be made out to say *tablet* if you looked at it just right.

"That makes a lot more sense," I replied. "Many people want tablets for Christmas."

Together, we managed to translate all of the items on his list. Then we had a good talk about practicing handwriting and spelling skills.

I left him with something to consider: "Can you imagine how disappointed you'd have been on Christmas morning if you found a toilet under your tree instead of a tablet?"

He shook his head in vigorous agreement.

Awesome Cookies

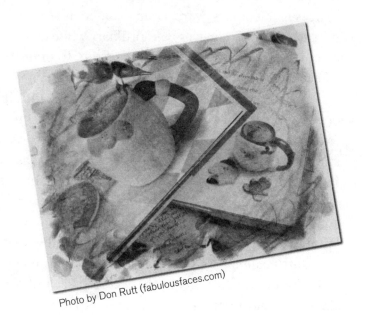

Photo by Don Rutt (fabulousfaces.com)

Working at my real job one afternoon in early December, I was sitting at my desk when a sweet coworker and talented writer knocked on my door. When I called for her to come in, I looked up to see Mary struggling through the door with a large platter of cookies. The cookies Mary presented to me weren't ordinary, purchase-at-the-store cookies. No. They were works of art. Mary told me that the cookies were made by a friend of hers who chose to remain anonymous. (Although

I had a good idea who my benefactor was, I have always respected the wishes of this generous person, and have not acknowledged them.)

The sugar cookies were hand painted masterpieces. The frosting foundation was extraordinary white chocolate that set off the bright, cheery colors of the decorations. I had never seen anything like these cookies before or since. To my amazement, each cookie represented a different segment of the poem "'Twas the Night before Christmas."

Many consider me to be an authority on the famous poem. I can recite it in both its original 1823 version as well as its modern derivation. I've studied its history for years and the minor controversy surrounding its true authorship. (I don't think Clement Clark Moore was the real poet.) It is written in anapestic meter and includes a number of distinctly Dutch elements. Regardless, the idea that someone would take the time to creatively decorate each of those cookies was, and remains, overwhelming to me. It is one of my great joys to bring the poem to life and share its rich details.

The cookies that were gifted to me were not only lovely to look at, but were delicious by any measure. In fact, Deb and I had a very hard time eating them—they were almost too beautiful to eat. But, we did eat them.

These cookies are one of the most special gifts in my life, which is why all of my Santa books—*The Bird in Santa's Beard*, *The Bump on Santa's Noggin*, and *The Elves in Santa's Workshop*—feature them. A gift from a dear friend I've never met.

Thank you from the bottom of my heart, secret friend.

Antique Cane

Photo by Don Rutt (fabulousfaces.com)

I enjoy wearing slightly different apparel than most who portray the Spirit of Christmas. Red wool pants with red braces and calf-high black boots (no buckle) cover my lower half. (Children often tell me they know that I'm real because I have real boots. Ah, the magic of belief.) That is where the traditional Santa ends.

Most of the time, I do not wear the red coat. Instead, it is purposefully hung on a coat tree near my chair. I also use it as a teaching tool to remind children to hang up their outerwear when they enter their homes. More importantly, the thick wool suit with satin lining is difficult to endure under room-temperature conditions. It is more comfortable, and more dignified, if I wear a shirt, tie, and vest. (For over twenty years, I've only received compliments on my Santa attire.)

Wearing a wool vest with lots of pockets makes visits more involved and more fun for children than a "Snap and Shoot" Santa. Generally, my vest carries a small flashlight (for teeth and ear inspections and finding my way around in the dark); an elegant magnifying glass (for close reading and storytelling); and an old pocket watch with a train on the cover, a piece that continues to amaze adults and children alike.

One of my other prized possessions is an antique cane that I purchased from a friend I've never met. More than a decade ago, I was scouring the Internet in pursuit of the perfect cane. As you may recall, in the film *Miracle on 34th Street*, one of the main props used by St. Nick is a cane.

During my search on eBay, an item caught my eye: **Antique Antler-Handled Cane.** Though I didn't pay attention to the point of origin, it was the perfect addition for my upcoming book, *The Bird in Santa's Beard*. It became apparent during the transaction the seller, Maurice, was a resident of Wales, a country in Great Britain.

I purchased the antique cane, and it eventually arrived from overseas. During the course of our Internet discussion, I learned of Maurice's occupation and a few bits and pieces about his wife, Jan. When *The Bird in Santa's Beard* was published in 2004, I mailed a copy to him to show how I had used this special cane. Even though we have never met in person, we have become friends through space and time, enabled by the Internet. And for nearly two decades, Maurice has never failed to send me greetings at Christmastime and on other significant holidays. In our correspondence, we always say that it would be wonderful to meet in person. Someday, I'd like to do just that.

A Special Timepiece

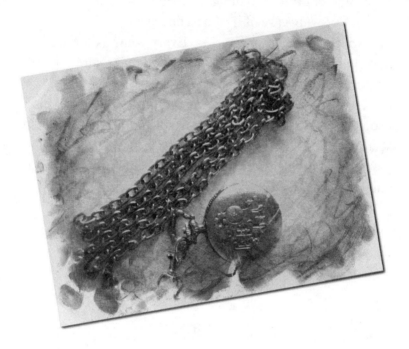

A close friend and valued coworker passed away from ocular melanoma at a young age. Prior to his death, I worked on a project for Walter. It was a unique display for an upcoming railroad industry trade show. After the successful conclusion of the project, Walter gave me a pocket watch as a gracious gesture of his appreciation.

The watch is a simple, stem-wound pocket piece in brass. On the cover is an image of an old railroad engine that is similar in appearance to The Polar Express. It is a plain railroad watch that means a lot to me and continues to delight the imagination.

I take loving care of it. When not in use, the watch rests in a special spot in my dresser. Every year, as the Christmas season approaches, I get it out and make sure it is still working. If not, off to the shop it goes.

This treasured gift is one of the most valuable tools I use to draw the interest of children of all ages. And I am secure in the knowledge that my friend Walter would be pleased to see how I use the watch in memory of a good and kind man.

Unusual Requests

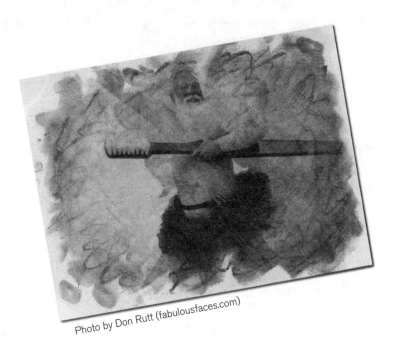

Photo by Don Rutt (fabulousfaces.com)

It never fails. Kids do say the craziest things! Although the majority of their questions and wishes fall into routine patterns, and the same popular toy or device is repeated thousands of times during a season, there are always several children who manage to come up with the unexpected. Following are some of the unusual requests I have heard.

Band-Aid—One memorable night, a little girl came to me with a simple request. Her eyes brightened as she spoke. "I want a Barbie Band-Aid for Christmas," she said. I thought about her request for a moment. "What would you do with a Barbie Band-Aid?" I asked. She instantly stuck her finger up between her eyes and said, "I'd put it on my finger and look at it, of course!"

Gum—So far, only two children have asked for gum. My follow-up question is: "Bubble or chewing?" I can't do bubblegum myself because of the beard ala Edmund Gwinn in *Miracle on 34th Street*. Removing gum from a beard can be a nightmare.

Candy—I can count the number of children who request candy for Christmas on one hand. Generally, I tell them I'll talk with their mother about it. Then, I take a moment to do a tooth check and offer a reminder about good dental hygiene.

Dirt—It seems like yesterday when I was visiting the Nate and Mary Ida Doan Santa House in Bay City, Michigan. Christmas music chimed above the excited churn of families waiting in line to visit Santa. A boy walked up to me and, after a pleasant exchange about school and reading, he told me he wanted a pile of dirt for Christmas.

I asked him why. He was very clear: "I've got all the trucks and tractors I need. Now, I want a pile of dirt so I can play with all my stuff."

When I asked him how much dirt he wanted, his answer was quick and precise: "Ten yards should do it." Then he told me there was a cleared space in the backyard where I could deliver it. As he was telling his story, I looked over his head. His father and mother were eagerly nodding their heads and giving me a thumbs up. When I told him I couldn't have it delivered on Christmas day, he told me I could have it dropped off early. Although I never promise anything, I am convinced a certain little boy got a truck-load of dirt delivered before Christmas.

Two Sheets of Paper—It must have had something to do with the alignment of the planets or some unusual rift in the cosmos. One year, two unrelated children asked Santa for paper for Christmas. Both specifically requested exactly two sheets. When I asked what they would do with two sheets of paper, the boy said he wanted to make paper airplanes. The girl wanted to use them to draw and color.

And, this is what makes sitting in the chair so much fun. Santa doesn't have a clue about what kids are going to say or request. I have the best job ever! Every day is an adventure.

What a hoot!

Asking for the Impossible

This collection of stories actually began with my memories of Danny. His requests were both generous and selfless (see "A Child's Heart" on page 3).

In the last decade, I have noticed a trend in requests for bigger, more meaningful things rather than toys and electronics. Many, if not most, of these requests are impossible to fulfill and can be a challenge to address—but they provide a peek into the hearts of children.

World Peace—In recent years, I've received several requests for world peace. Certainly children are being exposed to the frightening information dished out in the daily news cycle. Smartphones, iPads, and electronics are contributing both to the speed of news and also a limitless supply of gruesome images that can make children uneasy.

The children who request peace are often upset and deeply concerned. I tell them that Santa has a knack for toy production and delivery, and that world peace is out of his league. However, it is safe to say that world peace begins with the individual. So in these situations, I encourage children to do their best to be kind to one another and if they see an opportunity to wage peace, go for it!

Save the Dogs—Possibly a future veterinarian, a girl requested that Santa save all the dogs who were alone and living on the streets. I told her that I couldn't possibly save all the dogs by myself. However, I did suggest that we could all help by choosing rescue/shelter pets. We both agreed we had a job to do, starting that night. I'd recommend to all my friends that they should consider getting pets from shelters and she would do the same. If everyone pitched in to do the right thing, the number of pets without homes would be reduced. She seemed happy with the idea. (Immediately after my suggestion, she asked for an iPhone.)

Faith—I was working in a Santa House in a major city on Christmas Eve. As the afternoon wore on, many children came and went. The hottest toys and electronics dominated the requests—until something unique and powerful happened. One sweet young girl with an earnest heart had a simple, moving request. She asked Santa if he could make her whole family Christians. There was only one possible answer to this request. We prayed together.

Family—It was near closing time at the Santa House. The line slowly worked down and I noticed that the last family was somewhat unusual. The people at the end of the line were a man and woman with a teenage girl.

Teenagers can sometimes be difficult for Santa. Most beard pullers and scoffers are children who are in their teens. I steeled myself for the possibility of a difficult encounter. My assumption couldn't have been further from reality.

The man and woman were arm in arm as the young lady approached me. She jumped on my lap and threw her arms around my neck, leaning in closely to whisper in my ear. "For six years," the girl noted, "I've asked Santa to make my daddy come home. This year, he did. I came here tonight to thank you."

I said I simply couldn't take credit for such a miraculous, joyful reunion. All I could do was hug her and tell her that I had nothing to do with her daddy coming home. It was her love and persistence that made it happen. Years later, I still recall that special night with a warm heart.

Dreams do come true.

Bubba and the Three Doritos

Like it was yesterday, I clearly recall walking into the dining room of a local country club to greet the members before going to the beautifully decorated Santa visiting area.

At the club's holiday brunch, Santa is positioned in a photographic set placed in a cove at the base of a staircase. A mailbox for letters to the North Pole, some wrapped boxes, a Christmas tree, and some cloth draping form a cozy background for a picture. The focal point of the set is Santa's chair—and yours truly.

While greeting the members, I was captivated by the spirit of one particular gentleman. His eyes gleamed. (I must add that he wore the coolest pair of glasses I'd ever seen. Being an eyeglass and sunglass aficionado, I was naturally drawn to him.) His smile was genuine, heartwarming, gracious, and kind. I have no recollection of what was said during that first encounter, only memories of the proud grandpa and his grandsons, Henry and George.

As it so happens, the same families often see me year after year. This family was no exception. Thereafter, I had the pleasure of visiting with Henry; George; and their little brother, James, each year at Christmastime.

To make each year distinctive, I invest time trying to find something special to show and entertain the regulars: a naughty/nice app for my iPhone, a ring for Mrs. Claus that would easily slide onto a two-inch pipe, and other such nonsense. I do my best to make sure they have fun. And at the same time, I come away from the holiday season uplifted by the interactions I had with the boys and their jovial grandfather. One Christmas season was especially magical.

I made a few inquiries and came to learn the grandfather's name. A few keystrokes later, I gleaned some information about him. It didn't take long to figure out that this was an individual I would enjoy getting to know.

One morning, the three boys stumbled down the staircase and lined up in front of me. Henry, George, and James. I visited with them for a few minutes as Mom, Dad,

Grandma, and Grandpa gathered to participate in the annual family photo with Santa.

As the family gathered around the tangle of lighting and photo equipment, we laughed together and had a wonderful visit. When the photo session was over, the family gathered to leave. That's when I made my move.

Before he could get away, I stopped Grandpa for a private word. Calling him by his name shocked him. "I would enjoy sharing a cup of coffee to get to know you a bit, sir," I said.

That simple request sparked a deep and abiding friendship that exists to this very day. And, I pray it will continue long into the future.

Over time, I learned that the boys call their grandfather Bubba. In turn, he refers to them as his "Three Amigos." Naturally, I couldn't help but twisting the names a bit. That's how they came to be known to me as Bubba and the Three Doritos.

Happy or Sad

It was the year I first met Sophie and Owen. Sophie was a beautiful young girl with curly hair and a heartwarming smile. Her big brother, Owen, was a handsome lad and a bit quieter than his sister. You know, the strong, silent type.

After we got acquainted, Owen pulled his Christmas list out of his back pocket and shared it with me. We talked about the items for a bit, then I turned to Sophie. Her list was comprised of a huge sheet of poster paper folded over four times. She stepped back to show it to me. As the poster unfolded, printed across the top were the words: It's All About ... in the box below the title was the carefully written name: **Sophie**.

I laughed out loud. "It's all about you, little one," I said. Her beautiful blue eyes lit up, and Sophie nodded her head in agreement.

When little sister, Ella, came along, the cuteness quotient shot through the roof. At about eighteen months old, little Ella wasn't too sure about meeting Santa. Fortunately,

Photo by Scarlett Piedmont (photobyscarlett.com)

Mom dropped her in my lap as Sophie and Owen joined me for the picture.

Due to the quick action of the photographer, the family got the near-perfect picture they wanted. Seconds later, Ella got a good look at me and promptly burst into tears. Owen, Sophie, and I quickly put on sad faces. Once again, Scarlett, the crack photographer, snapped a great picture of all of us looking quite upset. It was hard to choose which was the better image—happy or sad.

As an end note, the three of them are now my dear friends. And even Ella is excited to see me at Christmastime.

Photo by Scarlett Piedmont (photobyscarlett.com)

Fondest Memories

Photo by Karen McClure

    I have enjoyed the company and professionalism of several talented photographers over the course of my Clausing years. My friends Don, Scarlett, and Karen are among my favorites.

    For several years, I was blessed to work with Karen, a kind and lovely lady who enjoys portraiture. During the months of October and November, she would decorate her studio with specific themes that made for unique child and family photographs with Santa. Those years, and the children I met, comprise some of my fondest memories.

Emily and I started posing for special Christmas cards and family memories many years ago. Then her sister, Sofia, came along to make even more perfect photos (as if that were possible). The two girls have been the source of many wonderful memories for me.

These days, the two are no longer young children. Emily is a talented dancer with an exciting and promising future. Likewise, Sofia is a young lady carving her own way through the world as she grows. My time with these sisters will always stick out as golden moments in my life.

Photo by Karen McClure

Acknowledgments

Photo by Karen McClure

My heart is full. Yet, it seems to easily make room for more love and more children each year. As I reflect on the memories in this book—and many others—I can't help but recall the people who have helped me give life to this extraordinary gift—the privilege of portraying the legend of St. Nicholas.

In this collection, I have already mentioned a few individuals who have added profoundly to my calling. However, I owe the greatest debt of gratitude to my wife, Deborah. She is my personal chauffer, coach, editor, and biggest fan.

Without her and her support, none of this would be possible, and none of these memories would have materialized in the first place.

My talented friends, Mark Bush, Don Rutt, and Ty Smith, freely shared their gifts with me. Together, we created *The Bird in Santa's Beard*, *The Bump on Santa's Noggin'*, and *The Elves in Santa's Workshop*. These three simple books continue to create memories and joy each holiday season. You guys are the best!

As an author, I am often asked what it is like to make a book. My response is, "It's the most terrible thing ever."

People look at me like I've lost my mind. I then proceed to explain that I have to get up early in the morning to meet my best friends in the world. We started working on the book and laugh all morning long. When we go to lunch, it seems like we laugh more than we eat. After lunch, it's back to work. All afternoon, we take pictures and laugh. Once the workday is over, I go back home for dinner, do some reading and writing, and watch a little TV before going to bed. Just before I fall asleep, I start laughing all over again.

If you do this type of grueling work day after day, your sides ache from all the laughter!! It's so much fun to work with good friends, especially when they are so creative.

There are also several amazing children who continue to inspire and encourage me. One is Amanda. We first met on the Santa Train over twelve years ago. At the time Amanda, was an infant. Years after our meeting, my wife and I attended a new church. Low and behold, there was Amanda; her sister, Faith; and their parents. To this day, Amanda remains one of my dearest friends. Her smile always makes me happy.

I could spend hours doting on other kids as well: Austin and Michaela, Gordy, Nicole, Jake and Joey, Elizabeth, Hayden, Harrison, and Emma. Chloe, Addie, Owen, Natalie, Stacey, and the students at Old Mission Elementary School also played important roles that have added to my personal visions on sugarplums.

Photos by Don Rutt (fabulousfaces.com)

Photos by Don Rutt (fabulousfaces.com)

And there is also Mike and his Pets That Pull who pitched in to make our stories so lively. Many of their photographs reside in permanent memory within my books.

God bless you all!

A few other young people merit mention as well. Nicki Peppermint spent several years as my special assistant. During the Christmas season, we'd dress up and visit a fine restaurant. Walking from table to table, I greeted people and told stories as Nicki passed out candy canes. As I close

Photo by Don Rutt (fabulousfaces.com)

my eyes, I can visualize Nicki Peppermint. She is dressed in her finest, with her hair in braids with baby's breath and holiday colors. An older man seated at a table looks at her and asks, "How old are you?"

Without batting an eye, her answer was, "I just turned four hundred. I get to be here tonight because I was voted Elf of the Year."

Nicki was also the head elf in the National Cherry Festival Children's Parade, leading the way for Santa and his security team.

In later years, Frank, the Elf on the Shelf, joined me in storytelling. One year his leg was in a cast and he had to scoot around on a cart. When children asked him what happened, Frank merely said, "I fell off the top of the Christmas tree when I was putting the star on it. Santa rewarded me by letting me come with him tonight."

The view from behind the beard exposes a beautiful side of life, a side that clings to the joy of belief and the wonder of imagination—a magical time that is far too short.

Portraying the Spirit of Christmas is a privilege and a true blessing. Thank you.

The Beginning ... Not the End

There are some people who think being Santa is silly. I beg to differ. What else can a person do to bring joy to people of all ages and create memories that last a lifetime? How else can a person exercise creativity and devise plausible answers to questions that are totally implausible? What else in life allows a person to peek into the dreams, fantasies, and wishes of little ones and the magic in their eyes?

With twenty years in the suit behind me, I can assure you, kind reader, there are many more stories I could share. And through the grace of God, I pray I will be granted many more years and given even greater opportunities to live and share stories.

Developing this collection has been one of the great joys in my life. I will keep these treasures with me as long as I live. If and how more will be broadly shared is not for me to say. It all depends on the whims and desires of a fickle marketplace.

Thank you for your interest and support.

Jeffery L. Schatzer
aka a faithful representative of the Spirit of Christmas

About the Author

Jeffery L. Schatzer is an award-winning children's author who has portrayed the Spirit of Christmas for two decades; visiting with thousands of children and families each year.

Schatzer has authored three Santa books, *The Bird in Santa's Beard*, *The Bump on Santa's Noggin*, and *The Elves in Santa's Workshop;* as well as the three-time national-award-winning picture book, *The Runaway Garden*.

Schatzer has also published a book on the Civilian

Conservation Corps in Michigan, *Fires in the Wilderness, A Story of the CCC Boys;* and a series of historical fiction chapter books for middle readers, *Professor Tuesday's Awesome Adventures in History.*

Naturally, he and his wife, Deborah, along with their dog, Dot, live at the halfway point between the equator and the North Pole.

Other books by Jeffery L· Schatzer

The Bird in Santa's Beard (2004)

The Bump on Santa's Noggin (2006)

The Elves in Santa's Workshop (2009)

The Runaway Garden,
A Delicious Story That's Good for You, Too! (2007)

Fires in the Wilderness, A Story of the CCC Boys (2008)

Professor Tuesday's Awesome Adventures in History,
Book 1—Chief Pontiac's War (2009)

Professor Tuesday's Awesome Adventures in History,
Book 2—Migrating to Michigan (2010)

Professor Tuesday's Awesome Adventures in History,
Book 3—The Underground Railroad (2011)